Supporting
Reading

More titles in the *Helping Hands* series:

Supporting Spelling by Sylvia Edwards, ISBN 1-84312-208-1

Supporting Speaking and Listening by Angela Wilson, ISBN 1-84312-211-1

Supporting Writing by Sylvia Edwards, ISBN 1-84312-209-X

A selection of other books for teaching assistants:

A Handbook for Learning Support Assistants: Teachers and Assistants Working Together by Glenys Fox, ISBN 1-84312-081-X

Assisting Learning and Supporting Teaching: A Practical Guide for the Teaching Assistant in the Classroom by Anne Watkinson, ISBN 1-85346-794-4

Supporting Children with Behaviour Difficulties: A Guide for Assistants in Schools by Glenys Fox, ISBN 1-85346-764-2

The Essential Guide for Competent Teaching Assistants: Meeting the National Occupational Standards at Level 2 by Anne Watkinson, ISBN 1-84312-008-9

The Essential Guide for Experienced Teaching Assistants: Meeting the National Occupational Standards at Level 2 by Anne Watkinson, ISBN 1-84312-009-7

Successful Study: Skills for Teaching Assistants by Christine Ritchie and Paul Thomas, ISBN 1-84312-106-9

Understanding Children's Learning: A Text for Teaching Assistants edited by Claire Alfrey, ISBN 1-84312-069-0

Supporting Reading

Angela Wilson and Julie Scanlon

Series edited by Sylvia Edwards and Angela Wilson

 David Fulton Publishers

David Fulton Publishers Ltd
The Chiswick Centre, 414 Chiswick High Road, London W4 5TF

www.fultonpublishers.co.uk

First published in Great Britain in 2004 by David Fulton Publishers

10 9 8 7 6 5 4 3 2 1

Note: The right of Angela Wilson and Julie Scanlon to be identified as the authors of their work has been asserted by them in accordance with the Copyright, Designs and Patents Act 1988.

British Library Cataloguing in Publication Data
A catalogue record for this book is available from the British Library.

David Fulton Publishers is a division of Granada Learning, part of ITV plc.

ISBN 1 84312 210 3

Typeset by FiSH Books
Printed and bound in Great Britain

Contents

For Andrew, Jeremy and Andrew

Acknowledgements

We are very grateful to the staff and students of the CACHE Level 3 Certificate for Teaching Assistants course at Yale College, Wrexham, especially Jane Gong, for all their help and encouragement.

We would also like to thank the publishers and authors who have been kind enough to grant permission for material to be reprinted, in particular Clive Webster for his poem 'The Sunshine Tree' and D.C. Thomson for the extract from *The Beano*.

Above all we would like to thank the children for their interesting comments and responses.

Chapter 1

What does it mean to be a reader?

This book is about reading. Its aim is to help you, as a teaching assistant, to support children in becoming readers. But what does it mean to become a reader? We would argue that being 'a reader' is different from being someone who 'knows how to read'. Of course, if you are a reader you do know how to read, but we probably all know people who know how to read but do so as little as possible. They have a very limited view of what reading has to offer them to enrich their lives. There are lots of reasons why they have got into this state and among these sadly we must sometimes include poor teaching in the primary school. We would like to examine more closely what it is a reader knows and does because we would surely all agree that our aim is to send children off at the end of their primary years not only skilled and confident readers but above all, as Margaret Meek once said, 'knowing what reading is good for'.

Are you 'a reader'?

Students at our college were often asked in the first week of a primary teacher training course to put up their hands if they would describe themselves as readers. Sometimes, alarmingly few hands went up – alarming because if we are to convince children that it's worth struggling with this very difficult activity, we must be able to enthuse about it as adults in the classroom. The children need to see us doing the things that enthusiastic readers do. What would you say if someone were to ask you that question? Perhaps you are thinking, 'I would have to say I wasn't'. If so, that may be for one of the following reasons:

- You have a wide range of hobbies and interests and don't spend all your free time curled up with a book.
- You hate being asked to read aloud.
- You're a slow reader – it takes you weeks to finish something.
- You never read 'the classics' of English literature.
- You don't like poetry.

If you have said 'yes' to any or all of the above, then can we ask you to reconsider your definition of what a reader does.

Time spent in reading

We must be realistic about the time children – or adults – will have available for reading. Reading can seem a quiet and solitary activity; becoming absorbed in a story can be so engrossing that it makes us forget where we are or what is going on around us. Many people – and perhaps boys particularly – don't find that attractive. 'It takes you away from people', one boy said when asked why he didn't read more. But a reader might only read in short bursts and hardly ever for hours at a time. Let's say that when the child grows up, one of the competing hobbies might be gardening. These days, a huge amount of gardening information is available on the Internet. A non-reader might ask the people she knows for advice but find no one with just the right information. A reader knows that a few minutes spent searching the web is likely to provide new ideas about companion planting or show within seconds where a rare plant can be located. Over the year, she might spend many hours trawling for information – but never for very long at a time.

Reading aloud

It's one of the strange things about the culture of a traditional primary school that 'reading' very often meant 'reading aloud'. Many students have told us how they were completely 'put off reading' by having to bring out their book to the front of the class. Perhaps it was from a reading scheme such as *Ladybird* (remember Peter and Jane who were always 'here'?) Then there followed an agonising few minutes while they stumbled through the next page, knowing full well that everyone could hear the mistakes they were making. Often, there was a piece of old Christmas card stuck in the back of the book, and the teacher would record the page the reader was 'on'. Some poor souls were 'on' the same page of the same book for weeks – much to the chagrin of mothers comparing notes at the school gate. In real life, enthusiastic readers don't often read aloud. If they do – perhaps having been asked to read the lesson in church, for example – there is always plenty of time for rehearsal. We should also add that nowadays we see far less of the excruciating 'reading a page to the teacher' (for more on what happens now see p. 60).

Reading slowly

Another agonising memory for many adults is of 'reading around the class' – a few lines each from the novel being shared by the class. No one heard what others were reading because they were frantically trying to work out which was going to be their bit. And oh, how tedious it was, as people stumbled through a particularly dramatic passage. In real life, it doesn't matter a jot how long it takes – as long as you remember to renew the library books. Good readers know that there are times to read fast and times to read slowly, and we need to help children to understand which kind of reading is appropriate for their current task. Of course, if everything takes a long time then reading becomes a chore.

'Readers' are people who like poetry and the classics

We think this is an elitist view and should be vigorously challenged! Of course, some of the greatest literature in the world has been written in English and as people who enjoy reading it, we hope we can entice others to enjoy it too. But some people like Marmite and peanut butter on their toast, while marmalade or honey is more to others' liking – and that's fine. This is not the place to argue whether or why George Eliot might be a 'better' novelist than Jeffrey Archer – both give a lot of pleasure to many readers. And there is something slightly dubious about the arguments that allowing children to read comics in the classroom is a good thing because it might 'lead on to something better' – it's not very clear how it's supposed to do that. It might lead to a lifetime of being hooked on comics. This is a limited diet but not life threatening. We firmly believe that in respect of *what* to read, we should be doing three things for children:

- Making sure that a wide range of reading material is readily available to them.
- Encouraging them to sample as much of it as possible and discuss it with others.
- Helping them to develop their own tastes as readers.

A range of reading behaviours

In the past, primary schools have perhaps been guilty of emphasising the reading of narrative (stories) at the expense of other kinds of reading. 'Oh, but stories are so enjoyable' we can hear you saying – and so they are for very many of us. It has been said that children should hear at least four stories a day to support their language development and love of reading. But although story reading and storytelling are a fundamental part of human life, life in the twenty-first century is a good deal more complex than that. Over the last 20 years or so, the National Curriculum and the National Literacy Strategy have emphasised that in teaching all aspects of English, whether it's reading, writing or speaking and listening, schools should be looking out towards the culture and society that children are living and growing up in. And they should be preparing them to fulfil a useful role in that society. If you remember the sixties with its emphasis on 'creative writing' then this approach might sound unfamiliar – even rather utilitarian. But it certainly need not be. In fact, it seems likely that many children, perhaps boys particularly, were 'turned off' reading precisely because they were offered stories and very little else. We need to provide a more balanced reading diet.

The twenty-first century world of reading

So what do people in today's Britain actually read? What is the world of print we are preparing the children for? You might find it interesting to keep a brief reading diary for a few days just to see how this question applies to you.

Reading screens, not printed pages

It seems very likely that this will become, if it hasn't already, the preferred option for many people, especially if they are hunting for information. If you are a successful reader of this kind of material (and we think it's important that you are) you will know how to:

- Use a computer keyboard.
- Send and receive emails.
- Access the Internet.
- Access a CD-ROM.
- Scan the screen to find what you need, avoiding the tempting array of distractions that will come up on the screen.
- Scroll up and down the screen.
- Use hyperlinks to take you further if necessary.
- Get back to something you looked at earlier.
- Save material, if you want to.
- Print a hard copy, if you need one.

How does this apply to children?

Children in the **Foundation Stage** (from the age of three to the end of Reception) work towards the early learning goals. The *Curriculum Guidance for the Foundation Stage* (DfEE/QCA 2000: 62–3) suggests that practitioners should show children how to retrieve information from computers and encourage them to see how their first-hand experience of the world can be enriched through ICT.

The National Curriculum states that in **Key Stage 1** (5–7 years) children should use ICT-based information texts (7a) and of course this continues into **Key Stage 2**.

Print-based reference and information material

Your reading diary will almost certainly contain references to some of the following (some of it, of course, could be done on-screen):

- Looking up a spelling in the dictionary.
- Consulting a handbook, e.g. *The National Trust Handbook* if you are thinking of going out for the day.
- Reading a leaflet picked up in the doctor's or dentist's surgery.
- Reading an education report, perhaps for an assignment you are working on.
- Consulting a recipe book.
- Reading a newspaper or magazine.
- Studying an advertisement for something you are thinking of buying.

As with reading a computer screen, you will have demonstrated certain skills as you accessed this material. If you wanted to check the spelling of 'occurrence' in the dictionary, you wouldn't start on page 1 with the A entries – you would use your alphabetical knowledge to go straight to the right page. If you knew which National Trust property you wanted to visit, you would use the index to find it. Alternatively, you might open the book at a certain geographical area and skim and scan through the pages until you found something that interested you. The leaflet from the doctor, on the other hand, might have needed slow and careful reading – to make a mistake could, quite literally, be fatal. You know how to adapt your reading behaviour to the task you are carrying out.

How does this apply to children?

In the **Foundation Stage**, children begin to get acquainted with print-based information by talking about the environmental print they see all around them. The *Curriculum Guidance for the Foundation Stage* suggests drawing their attention to words they see frequently such as 'EXIT', their own and their friends' names on their trays and hooks at school, and words such as 'open' and 'bus stop' (DfEE/QCA 2000: 63). You will find many opportunities to demonstrate the usefulness of print: make a point of consulting a calendar with the children or writing a list to remind you of jobs to be done and then let the children see you referring to it throughout the day. If a question comes up as you talk about something you have done together, even if you know the answer already, let the children see how you would go about first finding a text that might give you an answer and then using the contents page, chapter headings or the index to find the appropriate page (for more ideas see Chapters 5 and 6).

In **Key Stage 1**, the Programme of Study for Reading suggests that children should look at print-based information texts 'including those with continuous text and relevant illustrations'. Try to ensure that you share books with illustrations of different kinds. Perhaps in your class you will be able to help with the making of a photograph album or you could look at a map or a diagram with a small group. Aerial photographs, cross-sections, graphs and tables are things you have learned to interpret fairly easily but children may find them puzzling.

The Programme of Study for Reading in **Key Stage 2** suggests that children should look at 'newspapers, magazines, articles, leaflets, brochures and advertisements'. It's possible that your class teacher might plan to introduce the children to the idea of **bias** in some of this material, i.e. they shouldn't believe everything they read! Turning children into critical readers is a very important task which starts in the primary school. Even if the material is not biased, it may be aimed very specifically at a certain group of readers. You might be able to help the teacher by taking a group to discuss 'fanzines' or magazines aimed at girls or at people who ride or who are hooked on cars. What do these publications take for granted about their readers? How do we know that they are aimed at specialist groups? (See p. 99 for more suggestions.)

Diaries, autobiographies, biographies and letters

What would you choose to take with you on a train or as bedside reading? Many adults prefer 'real life' stories to fiction although we need to be careful with terminology here. There can, of course, be fictional biographies about invented characters, and sometimes novels are structured entirely in the form of letters. Many so-called 'true-life stories' are in fact extremely biased – or even full of lies. All these nuances can be explored with children at Key Stage 2. 'Faction' (a mixture of fact and fiction) has become a very popular genre – books such as *War Boy* by Michael Foreman in which the author tells the story of his life as a young boy in World War II. The book is as gripping as any novel, with fascinating characters and vividly described scenes and events. But the events are true and a child can learn a lot about the war from both the text and the illustrations.

If you have not been in a school for quite a while you might be thinking at this point: 'But I thought children learned to read from a reading scheme? This doesn't sound like the *Beacon Readers* or *Janet and John*.' Some of the more recent reading schemes have enlarged their scope tremendously to include the whole range of texts we are outlining here (for more on reading schemes see p. 42). It is certainly the case that the National Literacy Strategy has made it impossible for schools to continue to offer anything so restricted as a single scheme. One of the pleasanter tasks that will face you as a teaching assistant is to continually update your knowledge of children's publishing. Your school or local library should be able to get you started. (For information on specialist journals which contain reviews of new books, interviews with authors etc. see 'Further information on children's literature' at the end of this chapter.)

Literature

We're using this heading because it's the one employed in the government documents but please bear in mind the comments at the beginning of this chapter and do not feel guilty if your reading diary refers to Bridget Jones rather than Jane Austen. We are referring here to fiction, poetry and playscripts.

What do people who have become 'readers' know about fiction?

- They know what they like. This might mean the work of a particular author. One child asked after the first book had been published: 'Have you any more of them J.K. Rowling books?' Millions of others asked the same question and the rest is history.
- They might know what genres of fiction they prefer. This could mean that they search out historical fiction, spooky stories, humorous stories or animal books, by a range of authors.
- They know more or less what to expect from the book they have chosen. They want it to transport them to another time or another place, or they want to be able to identify with the characters whose lives

are perhaps similar to theirs. Or they want to be horrified or terrified from the safety of their armchairs.

● They have perhaps learned to love a particular 'authorial voice'. For children, it might be the irreverent and endlessly inventive voice of Roald Dahl – almost always on the side of the child against a host of very unattractive adults!

● They may take pleasure from the intricacies of the plot – a good detective novel, for example, keeps one guessing to the very end.

The list could go on and on.

Why do some people enjoy reading poetry?

'Goodness knows!' may be your immediate response and probably voluntary poetry reading is a minority taste, although many more people enjoy singing songs which could be seen as poetry set to music. There are aspects of reading poems that are not so very different from the pleasures of reading a novel:

– Poems, like novels, are shaped in some way but often much more elaborately or intricately than stories.

– Words are chosen with care and deliberately placed for maximum effect, even if this means that the reader has to struggle a bit more to understand the meaning.

– Above all, poems, like some stories, can have layers of meaning. A 'reader' of the kind we have been discussing in these pages can see meanings beyond the literal – can unpeel the layers of meaning like the layers of an onion. Each reader might see a different layer and sometimes the same reader, returning to a text after some time, interprets it in quite a different way.

– This might have something to do with the way a writer has used figurative language – metaphors and similes.

– A reader can see how this text perhaps makes references to other texts by the same or another writer – just as we can hear echoes of one composer in another composer's music. Sometimes this is quite deliberate on the part of the writer: s/he relies on the reader to pick up these references and use them to enrich their reading experience. A writer called Frank Smith once said that becoming a reader was like joining a club in which all the members have lots of shared memories and experiences that they are continually referring to. Great if you're an insider – but a bit mystifying if you're not!

How does this apply to children?

You may be thinking 'All this sounds more like my old O-level or GCSE English – not the kind of thing I'll have to tackle in a primary school.' If you are thinking along those lines, then you need to get hold of a copy of the National Literacy Strategy framework document (DfEE 1998) as a matter of urgency. (This document is now a part of the National Primary Strategy.) It contains a term-by-term list of objectives for Reception to Year 6 which covers the ground listed above but in far more detail. This document in turn derives from the National Curriculum.

Children's reading of fiction and poetry

In *Curriculum Guidance for the Foundation Stage*, you will find reference to the wide range of material that children should encounter (p. 44). This includes rhymes, poetry and stories. These should not be so much new material however that the children have no opportunity to return again and again to their favourites. This applies to all phases of schooling and it doesn't matter if sometimes a Key Stage 2 child wants to take home something remembered with pleasure from Key Stage 1. Sometimes all of us want novelty and challenge but at other times we want the opposite. Of course you need to keep an eye open for the child who *only* ever reads Roald Dahl, football books or the shortest book on the shelves!

Even very young children respond to the shape and structure of a story or a poem. You will know this if you have ever tried to summarise a story to cut the bedtime reading session down and have been told in no uncertain manner that that's not what it says! For example, 'In a dark, dark wood was a dark, dark house. In the dark, dark house was a dark, dark room' (Brown 1992) simply isn't the same if it is changed to 'There was a dark room in a dark house in a dark wood.'

Lots of nursery rhymes must be quite meaningless to children as far as the content goes. Who is the strange baby called Bunting for instance? Is that her first name or her last? We don't usually talk about 'Baby Smith' or 'Baby Jones'. And what, city children might ask, does it mean to say her daddy's gone a-hunting to find a rabbit skin to wrap her in? Is there no Mothercare where she lives? Nevertheless, in spite of these mysteries, children love the sounds and rhythms of the verse and are quite happy to recite it over and over again without question.

We talked about readers wanting a story either to transport them out of themselves or alternatively to take them deeper into their own world. The Programme of Study for Key Stage 1 insists that children aged 5–7 should experience the same range (p. 47). It also mentions stories, plays and poems by significant authors. If you are not sure who counts as 'significant' – and it is debatable – you will find the 'Further information on children's literature' at the end of this chapter is very useful.

Part of your repertoire of children's literature should include stories from other cultures. In multilingual classrooms you should find stories in other languages and bilingual texts. Sharing stories is a very powerful and enjoyable way in to English, particularly if the stories have a pattern so that even beginner readers can join in (for more on this see Chapter 5).

It is in Key Stage 2 that some of the demands on readers become much more sophisticated than you may remember from your own school days. We shall have more to say on this in Chapters 6 and 7. As far as the range of literature is concerned, you will find, as an addition to the range at Key Stage 1, long-established children's fiction and modern and classic poetry.

Summary

In this chapter we have discussed:

- Some of the demands that are made on readers in the twenty-first century as far as breadth of reading material is concerned. We have been asking the question: What makes a *reader* as distinct from *someone who knows how to read but doesn't find it very useful or enjoyable?*

- Current approaches to children's reading development, which stress the importance of offering children a range of material and of rooting their experience of reading in light of everything else that is going on in their lives from the very start.

◼ Further reading

Barrs, M. and Ellis, S. (1998) *Reading Together: A Parents' Handbook.* London: Walker Books.

Brown, R. (1992) *A Dark, Dark Tale.* London: Red Fox.

DfEE (1998) *National Literacy Strategy Framework for Teaching.* London: DfEE.

DfEE/QCA (2000) *Curriculum Guidance for the Foundation Stage.* London: DfEE/QCA.

Meek, M. (1990) *On Being Literate.* London: Bodley Head.

◼ Further information on children's literature

Books for Keeps, FREEPOST, 6 Brightfield Road Lee, London SE12 8QF
Carousel: the Guide to Children's Books. For more information contact David and Jenny Blanch, www.carouselguide.co.uk

There is a very good website managed by Booktrust to help teachers, libraries, parents and young people to find out about books: www.booktrusted.co.uk

Chapter 2

What's involved in learning to read?
1 Phonic knowledge and word knowledge

■ Cracking the code

Learning to read is a bit like deciphering a secret code. Babies and young children first meet language as a series of sounds grouped together to make a variety of spoken texts. Then, at about the age of two, they discover print even though it's a while before they can decipher these strange squiggles for themselves. The French philosopher, Jean-Paul Sartre, said that when he was a very young child, watching adults reading, he thought they were praying. They put their heads down over the paper and confusing sounds came out of their mouths.

If you are working in the Foundation Stage, you might need to discuss with the children what exactly is going on when someone picks up something to read. What are they looking at? How do they know what to do? You can find a useful list of suggestions for activities in the *Curriculum Guidance for the Foundation Stage* (DfEE/QCA 2000: 63) (see also Chapter 5 of this book).

■ The patterns of language

The fact has to be faced that the teaching and learning of reading is a complex business. There are many ways in: some children will find one way easier, some another. In the past, this has not always been fully recognised, sometimes resulting in the failure to enjoy reading which we talked about in Chapter 1.

Though we may each have our own preferred way of coping, nevertheless all readers will find it very helpful to recognise that there are four levels of language pattern in a written text. If readers can recognise common features of each of these kinds of pattern, they will be well on their way to under-standing the meaning of the text they are dealing with. The National Literacy Strategy puts it this way: literate pupils should 'be able to orchestrate a full range of reading cues' (p. 3). It refers to these as:

- Context cues (when a reader recognises a pattern in the text as a whole).
- Grammatical cues (when a reader can see the patterns in the sentence structures).
- Graphic cues (when a reader recognises a word on sight or sees it as belonging to a particular family of words).
- Phonic cues (when readers are able to break down written words into their constituent sounds).

The National Literacy Strategy also refers to these cues as 'searchlights', perhaps because each of them sheds light on the mystery of the meanings hidden in the text.

In this chapter, we will talk about phonic and graphic cues.

Decoding written words using phonic cues

Many people probably believe that this *is* what reading is. They might tell you that readers look at each of the squiggles we call 'letters of the alpha-bet' on the page of writing and try to turn them into something meaningful – perhaps aloud but, as an adult reader, more probably in their head.

Phoneme/grapheme correspondence

This way of trying to make progress with a text means breaking down each word into its smallest parts: the individual sounds. There are 44 clearly distinguishable sounds in English when it is spoken with the accent described as RP (Received Pronunciation) (for an explanation of RP see *Supporting Speaking and Listening* in this series, p. 24). If you have a regional accent, you may use the sounds differently from the class teacher or your pupils – unless of course you all come from the same region. And you may have a few extra sounds. If you are a Welsh speaker, for example, you will use the sound represented by the letters 'll' which can be heard at the beginning of 'Llandudno'. Each of these 44 sounds is known as a phoneme of English. To write these sounds or phonemes down, we use letters of the alphabet in various combinations.

Breaking words down into their constituent sounds and then putting them back together again is known as 'phonics' or a 'phonic approach' to reading. You may already know the terms the teacher uses for this:

- Breaking words down into sounds is known as **segmenting**.
- Building the sounds into a word is known as **blending**.

Here is a fairly straightforward example:

CAT

As an adult reader, you will probably have no difficulty segmenting this word into three sounds, /c/ and /a/ and /t/.[1] When blended together into a whole word – 'cat' – you immediately recognise the label for that furry group of animals, the specific example of which is known in your house as Tibbles. There are three sounds or phonemes, and a letter of the alphabet to represent each sound. Technically, we would say that the spelling of 'cat' contains three graphemes.

Is a grapheme the same then as a letter of the alphabet? Sadly, no, it's more complicated than that. Think about the word **knight** for example, and say it aloud

- How many sounds can you hear?
- How many letters of the alphabet are used to write the word down?

Hopefully, you have decided that there are three sounds: /n/ and /i/ and /t/. You will certainly have counted six letters of the alphabet. Graphemes here come in different sizes:

---

1   When letters are written between parallel lines (//) they denote a sound rather than a letter of the alphabet. There is a phonetic alphabet which enables sounds to be written down more accurately but this has not been used in this book except on a few occasions which will be explained in the text.

- The sound /n/ is represented by two letters: 'k' and 'n'. Two letters to make one sound is known as a digraph.

- The sound /i/ is represented by three letters: 'i', 'g' and 'h'. Three letters to make one sound is known as a trigraph.

- The sound /t/ is represented by one letter: 't'. This is known as a graph (not to be confused with anything in mathematics!).

You can already see that the phonic approach to reading (which is what segmenting and blending is known as) is a tricky business. Segmenting and blending are the most difficult bits for many people, not just children but also those adults who struggle with reading. This is especially true for anyone who is even mildly dyslexic (for more on dyslexia, see 'Further reading' at the end of this chapter). Dyslexics find it very difficult indeed to hear the constituent sounds in a word – it certainly isn't easy for any of us. How many sounds are there in 'together' for example?[2] And we are only looking at one of the hurdles, so far.

Let's go back briefly to the word **cat**. We decided to break it down into three sounds: /c/ and /a/ and /t/. But if your name is Celia you will know that the letter 'c' makes a /s/ sound at the beginning of your name. So a child reader called Cindy or Cedric might render /c/ and /a/ and /t/ as 'sat'. Does 'circus' sound like 'kirkus' or 'sirsus'? We adult readers know that neither of these is true. One of the difficulties is that there are 44 sounds in English but only 26 letters of the alphabet, so this is bound to make for some difficulties.

If you are working in the Foundation Stage or Key Stage 1 particularly, it will be part of your job to help the teacher to work on segmenting and blending with the children. You will find that the National Literacy Strategy framework document has specified the order in which the segmenting and blending of sounds is to be taught (DfEE 1998).

Reception

With these children, you will be working on all consonants in the initial (first) position in a word and on short vowel sounds. This applies both to

---

2   There are six, but the second and the last are that very obscure sound represented by ' ə ' in the phonetic alphabet. This symbol is known as a schwa. You can hear the sound at the end of 'the', for example.

the sounds and their written shapes. A few of the digraphs I mentioned earlier will come in here: /sh/ and /ch/ and /th/. The children in Reception should also recognise and name each letter of the alphabet and be aware of alphabetical order. By the end of their Reception year, the children should also be able to discriminate, write and read final sounds in simple words.

Year 1

The word 'cat' is an example of what is known as a CVC word – consonant/vowel/consonant. The initial sound is /c/ and the final sound is /t/. Children should be able to identify these two sounds when they are in Reception and by Year 1 should also be able to hear the medial sound – in this case, the short vowel sound /a/. Other examples would be /e/ as in 'pet'; /i/ as in 'pig'; /o/ as in 'hot'; /u/ as in 'jug'.

If children are taught to sound out indiscriminately, letter by letter, they will very quickly get into all sorts of trouble. Consider a very common word such as 'the' for example. Saying '/t/ /h/ /e/' would be disastrous. Even in Reception, children should have learned that 'th' and 'sh' and 'ch' are to be seen as whole units and not broken down further into their constituent letters (Christopher, of course, or Christine will have additional knowledge about 'ch'). In Year 1, children are shown that where words end in 'ck', 'ff', 'll', 'ss' or 'ng' these are also to be taken as whole units. (Some regional accents do actually make 'ng' into two separate sounds – in 'singing' for example, which in those areas is pronounced 'sin-ging'.)

Where two letters of the alphabet are used to make one sound, as in 'ch', 'sh' or 'th', we label the combination a consonant digraph. It is impossible to distinguish two separate sounds. However, let's take some other groups of words, for example:

- bridge – brown – break
- scratch – scrap – scrabble
- milk – silk
- lamp – jump – limp

It is possible, by listening carefully, to hear two or sometimes three consonant sounds at the beginning or end of a word. The sounds are very closely aligned but they are distinguishable. (In the examples above, 'br' and 'scr' are in the initial position and 'lk' and 'mp' are in the final position.) These are known as consonant clusters or blends, and children in Year 1 should be able to discriminate, blend and spell them.

By the time children reach the end of Year 1 you will find yourself working on a more difficult feature: long vowel phonemes. These are admittedly more difficult for children as spellers than as readers because when reading, the children can always find other cues to help them decipher the meaning (for more help on the spelling aspect of these see *Supporting Spelling* in this series, p. 67). We make the long vowel sounds in English in a bewildering range of ways. Dyslexics in particular struggle, as spellers, with which variant to choose. Take the long /e/ sound, for example. We can find:

● meat – meet – field

Long /i/ can be written as:

● fly – side – tie –dye – high

Each long vowel sound has a range of alternative spellings and from the end of Year 1 and throughout Year 2, you will go on to other vowel sounds such as /oo/ and /air/. Again there are regional accent variations to consider: in Lancashire, for instance, 'book', 'cook', 'moon' and 'soon' all have a similar medial sound. In RP, 'book' rhymes with 'cook' and 'moon' rhymes with 'soon' but the pairs are distinct. 'Fair' spoken with a regional accent can sound more like 'fur'.

As stated above, there are only 26 letters of the alphabet to serve our spelling purposes and combinations of letters have to work hard in lots of different guises. The vowel digraph 'ea' was doing some good work up above, in 'meat', but it turns up again in 'bread' sounding quite different. As for 'ough' – what a worker that combination is. We have 'tough' and 'cough' and 'bough' and 'ought' and 'through'. Usually, readers will have some help from the context in which they find the words, but for children as spellers there are difficulties.

Segments come in different sizes

Imagine you are sharing a book with children and they get stuck on a word. We cannot emphasise too strongly how unhelpful it is always to allow them to sound out the word indiscriminately, letter by letter. This can be frustrating for the children and what is worse, can result in them losing track of the meaning of the texts they are reading; their minds will focus only on the next letter and the sound it makes. Instead, you as the experienced reader, have a decision to make. Is sounding out letter by letter a helpful option? It might be if the child has a problem with a word with a fairly straightforward spelling – a name for example, such as 'Peter' or 'Helen'. However, even if you feel that word-splitting is the best option (and we will consider other options in the next chapter), there are other ways of segmenting than merely letter by letter.

Onsets and rimes

Consider this group of words:

● bread – head – lead – dead

You will have noticed a pattern:

● br ead
● h ead
● l ead
● d ead

This is a family of words with the same 'rime'. A rime, not to be confused with a 'rhyme', is the part of a word or syllable which contains the vowel and the final consonant or consonant cluster. The part of the word before the vowel (br, h, l and d) is known as the onset. In a case like this, if children can gain instant recognition of this 'rime family' it will be of much more use to them than splitting the words into /b/, /r/, /e/,/a/ and /d/ etc.

Here is another example:

● light
● sight

- tight
- might

The rime 'ight' needs to be recognised as a whole. Nothing will be gained by breaking it down into /i/ and /g/ and /h/ and /t/.

Syllables

It's easier to give examples of syllables than to define them! They are, in a way, like beats in music – you can clap them out. Think of names again:

> One-syllable names (monosyllabic): Anne, Charles, Guy, Chris.
> Two-syllable names: Mary, Anna, David, Steven.
> Three-syllable names: Christopher, Jennifer, Annabel, Josephine.

Sometimes, you will find that when children are stuck on a word the best way to help them is to encourage them to look at the word syllable by syllable, e.g. 'dinosaur', 'family' or 'children'.

We have mentioned three ways of segmenting words in this chapter so far:

- phoneme by phoneme;
- onset and rime;
- syllable by syllable.

Don't panic too much if you feel that there's a lot to get through in Key Stage 1. The National Literacy Strategy framework document (DfEE 1998) does have a lot of revision and reinforcement built into it and all this work can be consolidated and built on throughout Key Stage 2.

Decoding using graphic strategies

We can offer the same reassurance as regards graphic strategies: although a good deal of material is introduced in Key Stage 1, it continues to be revisited and revised throughout Key Stage 2. So far, we have focused on the smallest units of the language: the 44 sounds or phonemes. Sounds combine to make words and we shall now have some points to make about whole-word work.

Word length

You might find children in the Foundation Stage who have some surprising ideas about words. Some, of course, may have little or no concept of what a word is, and may write a whole text without breaking it into words at all (see *Supporting Writing* in this series, p. 18); other children believe that there is a physical connection between the size of a word and the size of the object it represents. So 'daddy' is a bigger word than 'mummy' because he is taller, or 'elephant' is a bigger word than 'mouse'. This may show up in the children's writing when they are at the stage of inventing spellings (see *Supporting Spelling* in this series, p. 9). It's important therefore to draw their attention to the length of words when you are sharing a book with them.

High frequency words

In 1969, some research by William Murray established that relatively few English words form a very high proportion of those in everyday use. It was calculated that 20,000 words form the vocabulary of an average adult, and of these, 12 key words make up a quarter of all the words we read and write. One hundred key words make up half of those in common use. Murray's research led to the publication of a reading scheme some of you will be familiar with – the *Ladybird Reading Scheme* (for more on schemes see p. 42). The *Ladybird* scheme looks old-fashioned in today's world, but of course it remains true that there are many essential high frequency words which children will need even to tackle very simple texts. The National Literacy Strategy framework has this to say:

> These words usually play an important part in holding together the general coherence of texts and early familiarity with them will help pupils get pace and accuracy into their reading at an early stage. Some of these words have irregular or difficult spellings and, because they often play an important grammatical part, they are hard to predict from the surrounding text. (DfEE 1998: 60)

What is being hinted at here is that these are not those exciting 'content' words which carry the meaning of the text and make it worth struggling with for a young reader. Exciting content words are words such as 'tiger', 'cauldron', 'helicopter', 'roar' or 'growl'. Rather, these high frequency words include many of the category known as 'functor' words; they are the 'grammatical glue' which holds the content words together. You will find a list of all the high frequency words which you are expected to work on in Key Stage 1 in the National Literacy Strategy framework document (DfEE 1998: 60–1). Here are a few examples:

they	said	who	many	again	would
of	because	your	too/to/two	once	
where	have	all	another	some	
as	took	much	from	what	

In addition, the list includes days of the week, months of the year, numbers to 20, common colour words and the names and addresses of the pupils/school. Ideally, children should come to recognise all these words on sight and be able to write them without needing to break them down into separate sounds. But once again, we would remind you that many children will not learn all these before they are seven – they will need constant help, reinforcement and frequent reminders in as broad a range of learning contexts as possible.

Families of words

To some children and adults who are struggling to read, each new word they encounter can seem like a totally new challenge. One of the most valuable things you can do, as a teaching assistant, is to help the strugglers to see the patterns and relationships in sounds and words. We have talked about some of these already, but at the word level an important concept is that of word 'families'.

Think about this group:

● Lea**d**er   **lead**ing   **lead**s   mis**lead**

All of these share what is called a 'morpheme'; the morpheme they share is 'lead'. Morphemes are what David Crystal (2004: 241) calls 'the smallest meaningful elements'. But 'Wait a moment,' you are saying. 'Didn't you tell us that sounds (phonemes) were the smallest units of language?' Well, yes they are. But 'h' or 't' or 'ou' by themselves contribute no meaning to a text. Morphemes are small but meaningful! There are two kinds: free morphemes and bound morphemes.

Free morphemes

The word 'lead'[3] quoted above can stand alone in a sentence and will convey a message to whoever reads it, as in:

- Who is in the lead?
- You can rely on the President to lead the country wisely.

Bound morphemes

As well as these 'solo appearances', the word 'lead' can be used as part of many other words. In the above examples, 'er', 'ing', 's' and 'mis' have been added on. These other parts of the words could not stand alone – by themselves they would make no sense at all. They are called bound morphemes because they can only be found attached to free morphemes. Once attached, however, they do significantly change the original word. Bound morphemes can be used to change the grammatical status of a word: 'er' for example changes 'lead' from a verb to a noun. They can also be used to change the meaning of a word: 'mis' attached to 'lead' implies that the leading is being done in a wrong direction.

Prefixes and suffixes

Another way to think about bound morphemes is as 'attachments' fixed to

- the beginnings of words (prefixes)
- the ends of words (suffixes)

---

3 Of course, we are aware that the word 'lead' can be pronounced to rhyme with 'said' and will then have a completely different set of meanings.

So 'mis' is a prefix and 'er', 'ing' and 's' are suffixes.

You will be expected to work on prefixes and suffixes throughout Years 1–6. The suffix 's' is a good place to start because it changes the meanings of some words in a very important way – from singular to plural in the case of regular nouns. Again, a lot of this has more significance for children as spellers (for more help on teaching the spellings of prefixes and suffixes, see *Supporting Spelling* in this series, p. 73). For readers, as we have said, the important thing is for them to recognise a word that belongs to a particular family: they need to be able to spot the free morpheme when the bound morphemes have been taken away. Another bound morpheme to work on in the early stages is 'ed' because it forms the past tense of so many verbs:

- called – wanted – helped
- heated – climbed – baked

Notice how differently each 'ed' can sound (/ed/ or /d/ or /t/).

Words within words

As well as spotting the free morpheme, you could also encourage children to pay attention to words by looking for other words inside them. Whose names, for example, can we see in 'patch' or 'tomato' or 'bent'? Sometimes words combine together to form other 'compound' words such as 'handbag', 'milkman', 'pancake' and 'teaspoon'. In decoding these, use the syllabic segmentation mentioned above. Each syllable is a word in itself and you can ask the children to find other examples for the word wall.

Don't be afraid of words!

Sometimes we have been saddened to see children reject a particular book 'because it's got hard words in it'. Of course, a book must be within a child's capabilities as a reader – perhaps reading alone or perhaps with help. Care should be taken to match the child and the book. But to be afraid of the odd hard word to the extent that a child puts the book back on the shelf is a sign of bad teaching. Even more unforgivable is if a teacher (or teaching assistant!) spots an unknown word and puts the book back on the shelf. Words are fascinating, not frightening. Sometimes, we don't know what they mean or we don't know how to pronounce them – so we find out. Sometimes, we will remember them and use them ourselves; sometimes we'll have forgotten them by the next day. The crucial thing is to encourage the children to become people who want to 'taste words' on the tongue and collect them and experiment with them. Most of the time, of course, it's more interesting to meet words not in isolation but in company with other words (and we shall have more to say about this in the next chapter).

Summary

In this chapter we have discussed:

- The four 'searchlights' or reading cues mentioned in the National Literacy Strategy:
  - context cues
  - grammatical cues
  - graphic cues
  - phonic cues
- Decoding using phonic strategies:
  - phoneme/grapheme correspondence
  - onsets and rimes
  - syllables
- Decoding using graphic strategies:
  - word length
  - high frequency words
  - word families
  - morphemes
  - prefixes and suffixes
  - words within words

Further reading

Cryer, L. (2004a) *Phoneme Track Workbook*. London: David Fulton Publishers.

Cryer, L. (2004b) *Word Track Workbook*. London: David Fulton Publishers.

Crystal, D. (2004) *Language A–Z* (Books 1 and 2), 3rd edn. Harlow: Longman.

DfEE (1998) *National Literacy Strategy Framework for Teaching*. London: DfEE.

DfEE/QCA (2000) *Curriculum Guidance for the Foundation Stage*. London: DfEE/QCA.

Riddick, B., Wolfe, J. and Lumsden, D. (2002) *Dyslexia: A Practical Guide for Teachers and Parents*. London: David Fulton Publishers.

Chapter 3

What's involved in learning to read?
2 Knowledge about texts

▨ What is a text?

We have used the word 'text' several times already and you may not be sure exactly what is meant by it. It's a more useful word than 'book' because it's more wide-ranging. As we discussed in Chapter 1, reading in today's world encompasses a variety of material, some of it very ephemeral (e.g. labels, posters and letters), some screen-based and some in more traditional book form. The material we read is linked directly with the lives we lead. So we can define a text as a complete and coherent passage of written (or spoken) material which comes about because people live in social groups or communities, and language is essential to them in living their lives. Each time someone, or a group of people, sets out with the intention of carrying out a job of work which involves making or sharing verbal meaning in some way, they are creating a text for someone else to read. (It's quite possible they may be only writing it to be read by themselves, of course.) Written examples might include:

- A postcard sent from a friend at the seaside.
- A thank-you letter.
- A college essay.
- A poem.

(If you would like to read more about what is meant by creating a spoken text, see *Supporting Speaking and Listening* in this series, pp. 17–18).

Nowadays, as we pointed out in Chapter 1, the National Curriculum and the National Literacy Strategy decree that all children should have access to a wide range of texts. The National Literacy Strategy framework document (DfEE 1998) is very prescriptive about what kinds of texts should be studied in each term, but your school may or may not adhere strictly to these guidelines. Prior to the National Curriculum, the main reading diet of many children consisted of the reading scheme perhaps supplemented by a class library of picture books or fiction for older readers. Nowadays it would be extremely unusual to find such a limited range though, of course, reading schemes are still in use (see p. 42). Many local education authorities offer an excellent schools library service and teachers can borrow a wide range of books including sets of books for shared and guided reading as well as non-fiction, some of it geared to cross-curricular topics.

Discussing a text with children

Even before children start to read a text, it's considered very important to ask them to think about certain aspects of how it came to be written at all. Questions the teacher might expect you to raise include:

- Why was this text written? What was the writer's purpose? What kind of material will I find when I begin to read it? Do I think I will enjoy it? Will looking at it fulfil my purposes as a reader?

- Who was this text written for? What kinds of knowledge and experience did the writer expect the readers to have? Do I have that knowledge? Will the book be challenging for me to read? Will it be very easy – too simple, even?

- Has the writer provided any support to the reader when it comes to accessing the text: are there chapter headings, an index or information highlighted in boxes for example?

- Does this text stand alone or is it a part of a series? Would it be useful or helpful to read something else first?

You will find suggestions for activities to help you address these issues with children in Chapters 5 and 6. In this chapter, we want to offer a few ideas about the thinking behind them.

Writers' purposes

Of course, a writer may have several purposes in mind when putting a text together. To make some money, for example! Lots of children have become much more aware of writing books as a money-making activity since the phenomenal success of the Harry Potter series. Usually however, this will not be your main topic when discussing the purpose of the text! Rather, you will be asking what kinds of meanings the writer was trying to make.

- Some texts are written as a means to an end. In a recipe, for example, the end in view is a successful bowl of pasta or a pudding etc. In a guidebook, the idea is to inform the visitors about what they can see around them. Of course, the writer can tackle the text in a number of styles. The guidebook can be humorous, for example, up to a point, but if it stops being informative and is merely silly, people will not buy it.

- Some texts are ends in themselves. We read them because we want to laugh at the humour, be puzzled by the suspense or terrified by the drama of the unfolding events. We enjoy the text for its own sake rather as we enjoy listening to a piece of music or looking at a picture in a gallery.

All texts, even very simple ones such as notes to the milkman, are deliberately constructed by the writer – they are not random marks on a page. Sometimes the texts are very cleverly constructed to contain layers of meaning or even to conceal the meaning. For example, we can read *Hamlet* many times over and probably not feel that we have uncovered all the layers. Sometimes texts are sarcastic or ironic – perhaps the writer's tongue is firmly in his/her cheek. Sometimes writers are biased or are telling lies – they may want us to detect the lie at some point or they may go to great pains to conceal it. Some texts look like narratives but are actually selling coffee!

Some of this text work will be difficult for children. Many find irony difficult to detect, for example. Nevertheless, it is very important that they meet as wide a range of texts as possible, and your support will be invaluable in helping all the children in your groups to access and enjoy them. Many children, even in Year 6, will get a lot of enjoyment from listening to you read a text to them. For the independent readers it is the pleasure of listening to a good reading, just as adults enjoy listening to something on tape or on the radio. For the strugglers, your reading gives access to texts which are too long or too tricky for independent decoding. You are keeping alive the pleasure and interest of reading for children who might otherwise be tempted to give up the struggle. Stories are most frequently chosen for reading aloud, but it's very helpful for children to have this access to other types of text, and to hear their rhythms and cadences.

Genres

This is a complex topic, but you may well come across the term and so we introduce it here. In the past, the word was used to group different kinds of literature. Narratives, for example, could be divided into the genres of detective novels, science fiction, historical novels and so on. Since the mid-eighties, the term has been given wider usage. Genres can be spoken or written and include 'any staged, purposeful language activity' (Christie 1985). By 'staged', the genre theorists mean that a text has a distinct schematic structure. All the texts in a particular genre will have a similar way of tackling the beginning, middle and end. We have already referred to recipes and seaside postcards, but genres also include sermons, knitting patterns, scientific reports and so on.

Another researcher in this area, Beverley Derewianka (1996) defines a genre as 'a type of text used in a particular culture to achieve specific purposes'. She goes on to say that each genre has a number of characteristic elements which are organised fairly predictably.

The work of the genre theorists has been very influential in this country – in the compiling of the National Literacy Strategy framework document, for example. It is likely to affect you most in that nowadays children in Key Stage 2 are expected to be aware of these 'distinct schematic structures' and 'characteristic elements' we referred to above – both in their reading and in their own writing.

What is meant by a 'schematic structure'?

Narrative structure

You will find among novels written for children, stories told in diary form and letter form, to mention only two. Try to include stories structured in as many different ways as you can as you read with the children.

Many stories are structured chronologically, i.e. events are described in the order in which they occurred. Children often write stories like this themselves, linking episodes together with 'then'. One useful thing you can do to help them is to show them, when you are reading together, the wide range of linking devices or 'connectives' that writers use.

According to Pie Corbett (2001), there are eight common story types: the wishing tale; the warning tale; the losing tale; the finding tale; the tale of a quest; the tale of defeating a monster; the meeting tale and the tale of fear. You can probably easily think of examples of each of these you will have met in traditional collections such as those of the Grimm brothers or Hans Christian Andersen, but the same types of story also crop up time and again in modern stories.

'Plot' and 'characters' will be major aspects in your discussions about all stories. A story typically deals with specific events happening to a named character or characters at a particular time. Often, the story starts by introducing the main characters and explaining something about the time and place they lived in. You will find a lot of references in the National Literacy Strategy to work on 'story settings'). Very soon, something happens to upset the daily routine and the plot develops from there.

In our culture, stories for children generally have a happy ending or a resolution to the problem. In traditional stories, the heroine was frequently married off to the hero. Nowadays it's not 'politically correct' to offer heroines such a limited range of options. You will come across many retellings of old stories where roles have been reversed, and a princess, for example, rescues a rather hopeless prince before sending him packing.

If you are sharing stories with beginner readers, it's very helpful to choose stories with repetitive or cumulative structures (such as *The Old Woman Who Swallowed a Fly*). This helps the children to join in with the reading, which does wonders for their belief in themselves as readers even before they can decode accurately. You can stop reading at an appropriate point and ask the children to tell you what they think will happen next. One of the exciting developments to watch out for is when they choose to do this using 'story book language'. So they may tell you that Mr Wolf is going to shout 'Little pig, little pig, let me in!' Or they may suggest that the queen will say 'Oh my! What is to be done now?' If this happens, you will know you are on the way towards turning the children into readers!

You will almost certainly find that children get enjoyment from the way a story is structured. The meaning and the structure – the way the meaning is made – are inextricably bound up with each other. When you are telling a story, rather than reading it, the structure may change slightly with each telling, but don't be surprised if the children pull you up and point out that's not how the story goes!

Non-narrative structures

Research has shown that in everyday life there are six frequently used non-fiction genres or text types; you will find these throughout the National Literacy Strategy framework document. You can read more about this research in a book by David Wray and Maureen Lewis (1997).

Recounts

In this type of text, the author describes or 'gives an account of' events s/he has participated in. The structure is often chronological. A diary or a letter to a friend is an example of this text type.

> Dear Jo,
> I must tell you about our trip to London. You'll never believe the things that happened to us. We left home at five o'clock in the morning, and the first disaster happened when . . .

Reports

These texts describe how things are, or were, at one time. You should expect to find that modern examples of this genre, if written for children, are more accessible than an adult 'report text' would be, though this is not always the case in older publications. Reports deal in generalisations though they often give specific examples. Whereas the subjects of the sentences in a recount tend to be 'I' or 'we', in a report text they are something impersonal such as 'the Tudors' or 'the water cycle'. *The Drop in My Drink* by Meredith Hooper and Chris Coady (1998) is an excellent example of a book adapted for the age and experience of the readers:

> Water trickles and seeps and flows. It freezes hard into ice. It floats in the air. It is liquid and solid and vapour. It is never still.

Procedural texts

These texts tell you how to do something, i.e. they give instructions. Again, you should look for the characteristics of child-friendly examples. Tesco include a 'Kids' Cookery Course' in their monthly magazine. Here is a typical extract from October 2001:

> Go Bananas.
>
> If you like bananas then you're sure to love this scrummy tea-time treat – it'll send you and your family banana crazy . . .
>
> Banana cake.
> This tasty treat would be great in your packed lunch!
> **Remember – an adult must always be with you when you cook!**
> Prep. 30 mins
> Cooking: about 1 hr.
> Serves 8
> Ingredients
> 125 g (4oz) butter, softened
> 50g (2oz) light muscovado or caster sugar
> 2 large eggs . . .

Explanations

This type of text explains how something works. There are some excellent examples of this type of text for young children. Here is an extract from *It's Disgusting and We Ate It* by James Solheim (2001) explaining strange eating habits.

> Frogs legs (Europe, America and Elsewhere)
>
> Imagine yourself slurping a soup full of tadpoles or finding a stuffed frog nestling in your rice.
> Today, most frog meat comes from the legs. But if you had lived centuries ago, tadpoles and whole frogs might have been your favourite foods!
> Frogs live in most of the world's countries. They are the only amphibians that live north of the Arctic Circle . . .

Presenting an argument/discussing an issue

These are similar and sometimes you will see them amalgamated into one text type. Put simply, the 'argument' is likely to present only one side of a case, whereas the discussion will put both or all the sides. The local newspaper might be a good source of an example. An argument was raging in our local paper for months about whether a new theatre should be built in the town and the issue gave rise to a lot of letters along the lines of:

> Dear sir,
> I am delighted to see that common sense has at last prevailed and that this foolhardy and wasteful project has at long last been abandoned...

Or

> Dear sir,
> What a tragic waste of a golden opportunity! At long last this town had within its grasp a feast of culture such as its citizens have been denied. And what is allowed to happen? The penny-pinching, unimaginative town council...

Whole texts or extracts?

We would like to make just one more point about the schematic structure of texts. We have already said that some texts such as stories and poems are comparable to paintings and pieces of music in that they have a pleasing shape. The relationship of one part to all the other parts is important. Readers cannot do justice to these texts unless they are read in their entirety. Sadly, the very requirement of the National Literacy Strategy which we might have been pleased about – the requirement that children meet a wide range of texts – has led to an outcome that we are not pleased about at all: the reading of large numbers of extracts rather than whole texts. Not only this, but because schools simply do not always have the range of texts that are called for, the children sometimes see only photocopied extracts, usually in black and white.

We must be realistic about this. Sometimes, it is perfectly acceptable to read an extract: adults will 'dip' into a reference book using the index or chapter headings, and children should be taught this kind of reading behaviour. Even a novel cannot always be read word for word. Nevertheless, as with a good BBC adaptation for broadcasting, children need to read or hear enough of the story to be able to appreciate its unfolding shape. Sometimes, where an extract has been used in the literacy hour, the book can be given to children to finish reading for themselves but the book may not always be within a child's grasp as an independent reader.

There is little point in mentally ticking off a genre as having been 'done' if the children are left baffled and unenthusiastic.

What is meant by 'the characteristic elements' of a genre?

Obviously, as with the above comments on structure, we can only introduce this topic here. You will find that in Key Stage 2 particularly, the teacher will be building lessons around some of the topics that will be referred to in this next section and you will be expected to pick up on those points and help groups or individuals to develop them in some way.

Some of the characteristics have been mentioned briefly already: one example is story book language – or languages, as there is more than one kind. They are significantly different from the ordinary, everyday language of 'getting things done' and children pick up on this very early and begin to enjoy using it in their own stories. Kaye Umansky in *The Fwog Pwince: The Twuth* (1991) makes fun of traditional story book language by deliberately contrasting it with something much more down-to-earth. This is the opening paragraph:

> **Once upon a time, there was a handsome young Prince who had the misfortune to offend a wicked Witch. In order to avenge herself, the Witch cast a spell over the Prince, turning him into an ugly frog.** (Umansky 1991: 9)

'Once upon a time', 'had the misfortune' and 'in order to avenge herself' all come from the language of traditional story books. But then Kaye Umansky goes on:

> Well now. Let's get the facts straight. Prince Pipsqueak certainly wasn't handsome. Oh, he was a Prince all right. You could tell that at a glance. At least, you could before he got turned into a frog.

In this extract, taken out of context, there's no language that couldn't be used by someone on the No. 52 bus talking about Prince Charles (apart from the last bit, that is). The humour of the book depends on turning the accepted plot, characters and language upside down, though the settings in this case remain the same as in the original – castles, woods and pools.

One of the characteristics of stories, as we have hinted already, is that they don't necessarily take the shortest route to the goal, as it were. You may have seen some very amusing one-line versions of classic novels and plays. There is a version of Chekhov's *Three Sisters* which consists of just nine words: 'Three girls want to go to Moscow and don't.' This is funny precisely because we know, as readers of novels and plays, that it's the journey the writer takes in telling the story that counts, not a bare summary of the facts. We are expected to live the experience with the characters. Very often this comes out clearly in the language of description. Some children hate these 'boring bits' as they call them, and skip them, but if they are to become genuine novel readers you will need to help them to appreciate the achievement in this extract, for example, from *The Secret Garden* by Frances Hodgson Burnett (1951: 60). It's the part where Mary, cross and contrary and at odds with everyone and everything, is led to find the key to the secret garden which will change her life:

> The flower-bed was not quite bare. It was bare of flowers because the perennial plants had been cut down for their winter rest, but there were tall shrubs, and low ones which grew together at the back of the bed, and as the robin hopped about under them she saw him hop over a small pile of freshly-turned up earth. He stopped on it to look for a worm. The earth had been turned up because a dog had been trying to dig up a mole and he had scratched quite a deep hole.
>
> Mary looked at it, not really knowing why the hole was there, and as she looked she saw something almost buried in the newly turned soil.

Why does the writer take so long to tell us that Mary found the key? It's because she wants us to enjoy reliving the experience; she wants us to feel that we are there, in that winter garden, looking, hearing and smelling, and sharing Mary's thoughts and feelings. Some readers will probably never appreciate these particular joys and will always prefer other types of reading material, but you can be sure that sharing texts like this with a group will help many children to enjoy them more. One boy, when doing a self-assessment of his reading ability, said that he 'wished he could stop skipping the boring bits'.

Beginnings and endings

These are always interesting parts of a text to look at. Sometimes, they are very formulaic, as with 'Dear sir' or 'Cast on 52 stitches', but on other occasions the writer can employ ingenuity and imagination.

Stories

We have already discussed one story book beginning ('Once upon a time...'); another frequently used one relates to the fact that in stories, the writer wants to bring his/her characters 'onto the stage'. So we might read, 'There was [an old woman]...' or 'Once there was...' The most familiar ending is probably 'And they lived happily ever after', though it's rather out of favour these days (as we discussed on p. 31).

Non-fiction

There are some formulaic beginnings and endings such as those that appear in various types of letter. Teachers are often very concerned to explain the rules which govern when to use 'Yours sincerely' and when 'Yours faithfully' for example.

Sometimes all the points in a non-fiction text are numbered or are in list form but it may be necessary to include a brief introduction and conclusion as well.

Sometimes subheadings are used, as in a recipe. There may be a short introduction to tempt us to make the dish, and then we expect to see 'Ingredients' and 'Method' and perhaps a list of the utensils needed and the cooking times and temperatures.

Children should have discussed the strategies used to open and close the text during the shared reading before going on, perhaps, to create one themselves.

The writer's stance towards the reader

In some kinds of text, we expect to hear the personal voice of the writer, speaking directly to us. This is particularly true in letters from friends, for example. We would be hurt – or very surprised – if they addressed us in a curt, impersonal way, e.g.:

> It has been brought to the sender's attention that tomorrow is your birthday and therefore this card is being forwarded to you...

What sort of birthday greeting is that? It might possibly be something from the bank manager (though mine has never sent me a text of this kind!). It certainly doesn't sound like one's best friend. Rather, we would expect to find something like:

> Hope you have a great day! I'll be thinking about you...

'I' and 'you' are from a group of words called personal pronouns and we would expect to see them in friendly, informal texts. You may have noticed that we have adopted this style in writing this book. We have never met you and therefore you might feel that it is inappropriate to write in such a friendly fashion, but we want you to feel that we are talking you through the issues, rather than adopting the more impersonal style which you might find in some textbooks and reports.

You might also have noticed that in the example above, the subject, 'I', has been missed out. (For more on sentence patterns, see the next chapter.)

We have discussed texts that are 'a means to an end', i.e. we read them because we want to make a chocolate cake or rewire a plug or build something from a set of instructions. A characteristic of these texts should be clarity; however, we've all wrestled with ones that weren't clear at all! The vocabulary should be precise; it may also contain some technical terms. Numbers, quantities, times, temperatures etc. should be unambiguous and easy to find. Sometimes, different font sizes or colours are used. Sometimes information is put inside boxes. Pictures, diagrams, photographs, maps and drawings are all crucial in helping the reader to reach the desired goal. You're likely to hear the teacher discussing some of these features during a shared reading session. You may then possibly be involved in helping a group to create similar texts for themselves.

In texts which are 'ends in themselves' – meant to be read and savoured like the extract from *The Secret Garden* quoted above – the vocabulary can be more colourful, perhaps making use of metaphors and similes to appeal to the reader's imagination. Flowers, says Frances Hodgson Burnett, have been 'cut down for their winter rest' – more colourful than saying that the gardener had chopped off the dead stems.

In humorous texts, and some texts written particularly with children in mind, you will find another type of vocabulary – slang. Slang is very informal and 'comes and goes' very quickly in the language. Hence you can easily make people laugh by using 'yesterday's word' for something. This is particularly true of 'youthful slang' which is difficult for anyone over 20 to attempt to keep up with! There are other groups who have their own shared slang – Cockneys, for example, or sailors or miners. Children's comics seem to use a slang which is from another era and frozen in time, but today's children still seem to enjoy it (see Chapter 7). In the recipe quoted above (p. 33) you will find the following examples of slang:

- Go bananas
- Scrummy
- Send you crazy
- Great!

All of these sound a bit dated – in fact, rather like the comic style we referred to just now, which may be just what the copy writers are trying to achieve.

Two other non-fiction text types we talked about were 'argument' and 'discussion', both similar to each other. The English language frequently offers writers a choice of vocabulary – words which are very similar in meaning but have different connotations. One of these words may be the 'unmarked' version – the norm or what we expect to see. The others will draw more attention to themselves, make us sit up and ponder on the writer's choice. An obvious example is the word 'nice' which is so overworked and 'normal' as to be almost meaningless; we encourage children to avoid using it and find an alternative. So the cake can be 'excellent', 'gorgeous', 'fantastic' or even 'sublime'. In the example we gave from letters to a newspaper, examples of emotive vocabulary include:

- delighted
- foolhardy
- wasteful
- abandoned
- tragic
- feast
- penny-pinching

Inevitably, we can only touch on some of the characteristics of a range of the text types which feature in the National Literacy Strategy and the National Curriculum. If you would like to find out more information, you will find some further reading listed at the end of the chapter. Just a word of warning. While developing as a reader does involve a growing sensitivity to 'the way things are done' in texts, the most important aspect of reading is the enjoyment and value the reader derives from the text. In the anxieties generated by the first appearance of the National Literacy Strategy, there was perhaps a tendency to 'quarry' the text to find examples of a particular characteristic genre feature on which to base a lesson. In fact, teachers were urged to do just that. As far as we are concerned, the enjoyment to be had from meeting the text (preferably as a whole and not an extract) and responding to its meaning are of paramount importance. What we need to be clear about is just how readers *do* come to derive pleasure from their reading. What exactly are they paying attention to? Then we can try to help those who are missing out on these pleasures.

The reader and the text

Perhaps if you are a Key Stage 1 teaching assistant reading this chapter, you might be thinking 'That all sounds a bit complicated. I'm glad it's nothing to do with me.' However, you would be wrong. As we said in Chapter 2, to many people's way of thinking, reading is 'decoding the marks on the page'. The argument we are building is that reading *is* exactly that, but we need to go further. Reading is encountering something interesting in a text. If children take off as independent readers, say, at the end of Key Stage 1 then, in Key Stage 2, they can find these interesting encounters for themselves. They can decode the marks and begin to get into the meaning. Earlier than that, beginner readers need someone else to help them to get at the meaning while they continue to struggle with the decoding. As stated above, patterned, repetitive texts are fun at this stage because memory can compensate for partial decoding skills. Then gradually, young readers begin to see likenesses and similarities in texts: they approach a new text with expectations derived from previous reading experiences.

Some children have been so 'overdosed' on phonic approaches to reading that they have lost sight of the fact that the text should make sense (see Chapter 1). The following is an example of what can go wrong.

Paul's dad is a farmer. He drives a big tractor.

Imagine Stephen, who lives on a farm himself and knows all about tractors, trying to read this text. An indication that something has gone badly wrong is when Stephen reads 'Paul's – dad – is – a – farmer. – He – dives – a – big – [long pause, no suggestion]' The gaps indicate a staccato, word-by word delivery, with no expression and no flow. The child is attacking the text a word at a time. He is focusing on decoding, but misses the consonant cluster at the beginning of 'drives'. The word 'farmer' should have acted as a trigger, so that the child's own experience could help him to correct his mistake and have a go at 'tractor' but he is not connecting with the meaning and therefore grinds to a halt. He appears not to have been taught to look forward and to look back, though at least his word 'dives' fits grammatically into the slot. It would be even more worrying if he had offered a noun instead.

Reading is an active process

The writing system and the spelling system are fixed, but meaning-making is not – or not always. Making a text mean something involves entering into a relationship with it. Of course, this doesn't apply to something such as:

Two pints please!

There are times, as we said above, when absolute clarity and precision are all-important. But there are many occasions when what the reader takes from the page is conditioned, not only by previous reading experience but also by such things as age, experience of life, knowledge about the writer and so on. This is where we find the excitement of reading. As we become used to reading a particular type of text we build up pleasurable anticipation of what we expect to find in each new example. We bring this knowledge and experience to bear in creating its meaning in our own minds, though of course it would be a very poor reader who deliberately ignored the cues the writer has provided. To be a good reader means to set up a dialogue with the text inside one's own head, with the words the writer has provided sparking off pictures, ideas, comparisons and so on. We think that this dialogue should be there from the beginning. The *Curriculum Guidance for the Foundation Stage* (DfEE/QCA 2000) seems to echo this demand, asking, for example, that young children begin to acquire favourite stories.

Reading schemes

It's very rarely that a reading scheme book becomes a child's favourite text, which should be a warning to us to ensure that the children's reading experience ranges much more widely. Nowadays, the publishers of reading schemes are very much aware of the breadth of reading material that is required by the National Curriculum and the National Literacy Strategy and most claim to offer examples of all the various text types we have been describing in this chapter, at each and every level of the scheme. Some of the texts will be in rhyme or patterned in some other way. Usually part of the scheme consists of a series of story books in which children meet the same characters again and again, hopefully motivating the children to want to find out more about them. Some of the stories are homely and familiar while others take off into the realms of fantasy.

This may all sound quite promising, but it has to be remembered that scheme books are written within tight constraints (see below) and sometimes, however good the intentions, the books lack the richness of language and illustration to be found in the rest of children's publishing.

Nevertheless, reading schemes do have a part to play in turning children into independent readers. Perhaps the teacher will ask you to do some one-to-one reading with a child from a scheme book, though with the advent of shared and guided reading (see Chapter 5) some schools find it difficult to fit this in. You will find that there are lots of supplementary materials you can use alongside the books: CD-ROMS, cassettes, videos, games etc.

There are many schemes available and you may well find that your school has 'mixed and matched' several of them. The teachers may mix some non-scheme books, which they have previously graded for difficulty, with books from the scheme. (The non-scheme books are sometimes confusingly referred to as 'real books'.) Reading schemes are expensive to replace and hence you may occasionally find some rather old material in the book boxes. In particular, be on the lookout for any books which present limited or negative images of women or people from other cultures.

How can reading schemes help?

The books are staged in order of difficulty with several titles at each stage for those who need extra practice. Sometimes the stages are numbered or they might be letter or colour coded.

What kinds of stages are we referring to?

Phonic patterns
If you have read Chapter 2, you will remember that we referred to the National Literacy Strategy framework document (DfEE 1998) and its recommendations for taking children gradually through the sounds of English and their written equivalents. CVC words, for example, with short vowel sounds, were among the earliest phonic patterns to be introduced. You will find that many of the words used at each stage in a reading scheme are designed to parallel the gradual progression of phonics teaching.

Sight vocabulary: high frequency words and families of words
The National Literacy Strategy also makes clear what words children should be able to recognise on sight at each stage of their development. These too will gradually be incorporated into the stages of the scheme so that children come to recognise them instantly, in context, without the need to segment them into sounds.

Sentence patterns

These will be discussed in more detail in the next chapter, but the principle is the same. The writers of the scheme will try to ensure that the sentence patterns become gradually more complex. Direct speech, for example, will only be included at an appropriate level.

Font size and style

As the scheme progresses you may find that font size becomes smaller and a greater range of font styles is used. It must be a difficult job to write a series of books within the constraints of maintaining the graded levels of difficulty outlined above. We have seen how the Department for Education and Skills (DfES) is urging that children should be encouraged to exploit all the cue systems as fully as possible. Nowadays, writers of schemes do try to offer children access to all the kinds of support we have been outlining. In older schemes, *either* phonics *or* 'Look and Say'[1] tended to be used almost exclusively. This exclusiveness gave rise to some very strange texts indeed. Given the task of constructing a book almost entirely around the sound /ur/ for instance, someone came up with a story about a hermit's purple shirt. It was bizarre. Nowadays, writers of scheme books strive for much more natural language and interesting plots.

Changes in the way reading is taught, and especially the introduction of shared reading (see Chapter 5), mean that the reading scheme has a diminished role (there is no mention of reading schemes in the National Curriculum or the National Literacy Strategy). Words can be introduced even in the early stages of teaching reading which fall outside the strict developmental pattern of the reading scheme. These are often the more exciting words such as 'rhinoceros' – the ones that children will respond to and remember because they make reading fun.

A balance needs to be struck between on the one hand, taking children gradually through the perceived steps to full reading competence, checking on their achievements at each stage, and on the other, allowing them to plunge into the exciting world of books so that they want to know more. The former may help to give them the skills needed to become independent readers, but the latter will turn them into people who want to read.

---

1 'Look and Say' is the name given to learning to recognise words, especially high frequency words, without breaking them down into their constituent parts.

Summary

In this chapter we have discussed:

- A definition of 'text'.
- The range of text types children are expected to encounter to fulfil National Curriculum requirements.
- Some of the ways texts are structured.
- Some characteristic elements of a range of texts.
- The relationship between the reader and a text.
- Reading schemes.

Further reading

Burnett, F. Hodgson (1951) *The Secret Garden.* London: Puffin.

Christie, F. (1985) *Language and Education.* Oxford: Oxford University Press.

Coghlan, S., Fitzpatrick, M. and O'Dea, L. (2001) *Changing Faces, Changing Places: A Guide to Multicultural Books for Children.* Dublin: O'Brien Press.

Corbett, P. (2001) *How to Teach Fiction Writing at Key Stage 2.* London: David Fulton Publishers.

Derewianka, B. (1996) *Exploring the Writing of Genres.* Royston: UKRA.

DfEE (1998) *National Literacy Strategy Framework for Teaching.* London: DfEE.

DfEE/QCA (2000) *Curriculum Guidance for the Foundation Stage.* London: DfEE/QCA.

Gamble, N. and Yates, S. (2002) *Exploring Children's Literature: Teaching the Language and Reading of Fiction.* London: Paul Chapman Publishing.

Hooper, M. and Coady, C. (1998) *The Drop in My Drink.* London: Frances Lincoln.

Meek, M. (1998) *How Texts Teach What Readers Learn.* Stroud: The Thimble Press.

Solheim, J. (2001) *It's Disgusting and We Ate It: True Food Facts from Around the World and Throughout History.* New York: Aladdin Paperbacks.

Umansky, K. (1991) *The Fwog Pwince: The Twuth.* London: Puffin.

Wray, D. and Lewis, M. (1997) *Extending Literacy: Children Reading and Writing Non-fiction.* London: Routledge.

Chapter 4

What's involved in learning to read?
3 Knowledge about sentences

So far we have discussed:

- the 'big shapes' that readers will meet – the texts;
- the smallest shapes – the graphemes which represent the sounds of the language and build into words.

Recognising the patterns at both these levels is essential to becoming a reader. But there is another level of language pattern. Words combine together, usually into sentences, according to another set of rules: the rules of syntax. If someone stopped you in the street and asked you what you know about the rules of syntax, you might be tempted to say 'Nothing at all.' In fact, you know a lot although it's 'implicit' rather than 'explicit' knowledge. You may find it hard to say what it is you know but you can use the knowledge without thinking.

Test yourself!

1. What word could you put in the gap in these sentences?

The girl . . . after the ball.

I love my new . . . trousers.

'. . . you going shopping this morning?' asked my sister.

In the first example, you will almost certainly have put a verb, a 'doing' word of some kind (probably 'ran' though many others would fit). You probably put it in the past tense, as if you were telling someone after the event, though you could have imagined you were watching her:

The girl runs after the ball.

Or you could have been describing something that is going to happen:

> The girl will run after the ball.

In the second example, the space is left before the noun 'trousers' so the word is going to be something describing them – an adjective. There are lots of possibilities such as a colour word or a word for the fabric: 'red trousers' or 'velvet trousers'.

In the third example, the word must be 'are' (or just possibly 'were') because you know that this is the way to structure this type of question.

2. Which of the sentences below sound correct to you?

> Joan carefully placed the jar on the shelf.
>
> Joan the jar carefully placed on the shelf.
>
> Joan placed the jar on the shelf carefully.
>
> Placed jar Joan shelf on the carefully the.

You probably had no difficulty in accepting the first example as correct; the second sounds a bit odd and is unlikely to occur; the last we're sure you rejected as total gibberish. The third, like the first, is quite correct. Adverbs such as 'carefully' can be moved around in a sentence, sometimes because the writer wants to place the emphasis in a particular way.

3. Could any of the words be deleted from the correct sentences above without destroying the sense?

The word 'carefully' (an adverb) could be deleted: the others are essential for the sentence to be grammatical (it could, of course, be expressed in note form).

So, perhaps now you will begin to rate your syntactic knowledge more highly!

Children have learnt most of the basic sentence patterns of English by the time they are five. As stated on page 41, had Stephen (who misread 'dives' for 'drives') put a noun into that slot instead of a verb it would have been more worrying. If he was totally confused and not making any sort of sense he might have read: 'Paul's dad is a farmer. He diver a . . . '

The very first sentence level objective for Reception children in the National Literacy Strategy is:

● Pupils should be taught to expect written text to make sense and to check for sense if it does not.

And the second is:

● Pupils should be taught to use awareness of the grammar of a sentence to predict words during shared reading.

The robot-like way in which Stephen reads is another indicator that he is seeing the sentences a word at a time rather than as a grammatical whole. Children who read like this cannot put the appropriate expression and intonation into their reading. Do try to break children of the 'robotic habit' if you come across it when you are sharing a book. Of course, to get them to read with expression also means paying attention to punctuation marks – not only commas and full stops but question and exclamation marks as well. As they progress to texts containing direct speech, they will need to notice speech marks or speech in bubbles. They should also be aware of text that has been written in bold or italicised print, wobbly lines or zigzag lines – the latter two are often used in comics to indicate how a passage should be read.

Because children know the rules of syntax (implicitly) it is possible for them to appear to comprehend a text and answer questions on it correctly without really engaging with the meaning. Comprehension questions should be phrased in such a way that this is impossible, but sadly some of them are not. To illustrate what we mean, read the passage below and try to answer the questions:

The fliber grippled the lemstock delmingly. The lemstock swengled. The fliber pritted. Eventually, the lemstock champed.

Q1. What did the fliber do to the lemstock?
Q2. How did the fliber do it?
Q3. What was the response from the lemstock?
Q4. What was the second thing the fliber did?
Q5. What was the final outcome of the fliber's efforts?

In Q1 you know that 'grippled' is what the fliber did because it has the regular past tense ending of 'ed'. So does 'swengled' – what the lemstock did in reply. In Q2 you know that the fliber grippled delmingly, again because of the word ending – many adverbs (words that tell us how things were done among other things) end in 'ly'. In Q5 the connective word 'eventually' gives you a clue that time passed and then, after some pritting from the fliber, there was an outcome – the lemstock champed.

All of this is totally meaningless. It may seem like a bit of fun, but many of us have probably got through an English homework by doing just this. We may never even have read the whole text – just searched for words that matched those in the question. This is not reading as we are urging you to see it in this book, nor are the answers an adequate test of reading ability (for more on this, see Chapter 8).

Children learn their knowledge about syntax first from the spoken forms, but as we explained in Chapter 2, the structure of spoken English is not identical with that of written, so there is more learning to do when they start to encounter varieties of written texts. However, we should never underestimate the huge amount that children have discovered about language before they start learning to read. We should take every opportunity to help them to apply this learning to the reading process.

Sentences

Many, but by no means all, written texts are written in sentences. Those that are not include lists and notices such as 'Keep out!' or EXIT. Sometimes, as we saw on page 38, informal texts omit some part of the sentence as in 'Thinking of you' or 'Bye for now!'

What is a sentence?

Sentences are not actually easy to define. We tend to tell children that they 'begin with a capital letter and end with a full stop' but this says nothing at all about what comes in between. In the National Literacy Strategy framework document (Year 4 Term 3) teachers are required to show pupils 'how the grammar of a sentence alters when the sentence type is altered'.

Sentences fulfil four functions. They can be used:

- to make statements;
- to ask questions;
- to give instructions (or these might be expressed more strongly as orders or commands);
- to utter exclamations.

All of these can be positive or negative. Here are some examples from a range of text types:

> Little Red Riding Hood set off for her grandmother's house. (Statement/positive)

Statements are often used for telling or explaining, so we would expect to find plenty of them in stories.

> 'Why have you got such big teeth, grandmother?' (Question/positive)

Questions imply someone asking and someone to answer – so again, they will be a feature of narratives. You might also show children how sometimes writers address their readers directly, as in:

> Would you like to make a delicious teatime treat for your family?

This might be a good way of introducing a recipe. The recipe itself is likely to be in this form:

> Cut some bacon into small pieces. Fry them gently.

Verb forms such as 'cut' and 'fry', which are telling the reader what to do, are said to be in the imperative mood. The grammar of English allows us to make many choices as we write. For example, instructions can be uttered very tentatively:

> Would it be a good idea to cut some bacon into small pieces?

Or they can be given with great force:

> Cut some bacon into small pieces! Do it now!

You can help to draw children's attention to variables like these when you are reading with them, and encourage them to try out a variety of forms for themselves in their own writing. Of course, they need to be aware of the consequences of their choices – some are not just forceful, they are downright rude.

Football team soundly beaten!!!

This exclamation is likely to be the heading of a newspaper article. It would probably be even larger in size. Notice also how some words have been omitted – possibly 'our' or 'the' at the beginning, and also the verb, which could have been 'were' or 'have been'.

The writers of reading schemes, as we have said, try hard to introduce children to sentences of carefully graded difficulty. They also aim to give plenty of experience of a particular sentence shape within a text. The most straightforward way of making a statement is in a subject/verb/object sentence. They look like this:

The dog (subject)   bit (verb)   the man (object)

One of the features that makes reading scheme books sound a bit odd is the endless repetition of this sentence pattern. Here is an example of a whole text, where the writer has also tried to use a limited vocabulary to help the beginner reader:

> Sam saw a parrot.
> Sam saw a flag.
> Sam saw a sword.
> Sam saw a hat.
> Sam saw a pirate.
> Sam saw Rosie.

This is certainly not a gripping text, but the repetition does give a beginner the confidence to attempt to read it, and if the final words are giving trouble there are picture clues as well.

Perhaps the next step in the scheme would be to introduce pronouns (for more explanation of these, see p. 55). Otherwise, the syntax remains the same:

> Jabeen saw her new kameez.
> She saw her new shalwar.
> She saw her new sandals.
> She saw her new bangles.

Again there will be picture clues for additional support and many children will also be able to apply personal knowledge to help them read the text.

A bit further on in the scheme direct speech will be introduced with its special punctuation features. Once we have direct speech we are also likely to have more examples of elision (letters omitted), which call for the use of the apostrophe.

> 'I'll take you to the zoo if you're able to behave yourselves,' Uncle Peter promised.

Children sometimes find the elided forms a bit tricky at first ('I'll' and 'you're'). It's well worth pausing to talk about the apostrophe as the correct use of these seems to be declining rapidly!

In later stages still of a reading scheme (and in other texts too, of course) you will find the indirect form of speech:

> Uncle Peter promised that he would take them to the zoo if they were able to behave themselves.

Joining sentences together

If we go back to Sam and Jabeen for a moment, another aspect of the texts that seems odd is their list-like quality. Usually, the statements would be linked in some way:

> Sam saw a parrot. Then Sam saw a flag. After that Sam saw a sword. In a little while, Sam saw a hat. Next, Sam saw a pirate. At last, Sam saw Rosie.

These words and phrases are called 'connectives' or 'linking words' in the National Literacy Strategy:

- Then
- After that
- In a little while
- Next
- At last

Again, by introducing the idea of being 'connective detectives' you can encourage children to search for more examples. Some children will even try using them in their own writing, but without a lot of encouragement most will stick to good old 'then'. In recipes and instructions, connectives sometimes take the form of numbers or bullet points, and you could certainly encourage children to use those where appropriate. There is one group of words, conjunctions, whose only job is to join other words together: examples are 'and' and 'but'. In one lively grammar video we came across, there was a character called Connie Conjunction who ran a dating agency for lonely words! It seems a great idea for helping children to remember the work these words do in a sentence.

Word classes or parts of speech

Conjunctions are not the only kinds of words you may find yourself talking about as you share books with children. The National Literacy Strategy also mentions:

- Nouns
- Pronouns
- Adjectives
- Verbs
- Adverbs

As we have said already, several times, there's quite a lot to take on board in tackling all these and we can only offer some introductory comments here (there are some further reading suggestions at the end of the chapter).

The work words do

In some cases, words can take on a variety of work depending on their place in a sentence and their relationship with other words. For example, in the sentence 'Are you afraid, Little Bear?' the word 'Bear' is a noun – a proper noun because it is the name of a specific bear. But in the sentence 'She had to bear the burden of her guilt for evermore', the word 'bear' is a verb. Then we can find it in yet another role: 'Toby gave me a bear hug.' Here the word 'bear' is functioning as an adjective, telling us more about 'hug'.

Nouns

On page 52 we gave an example of the simplest kind of statement. It had three parts:

subject	verb	object
Sam	saw	Rosie

Very often, the slots for the subject and the object in a sentence are filled by words behaving as nouns. Nouns are used by writers (and speakers) to name people, things, actions and ideas. They can be grouped into two divisions: proper and common. Common nouns are divided into 'count' or 'non-count' types, both of which can provide concrete or abstract examples. A proper noun is the name of a specific person or place, or perhaps a special time such as 'Christmas'. Proper nouns are written with a capital letter, as in 'Toby'. Count nouns refer to individual items such as hats or pirates. Non-count nouns refer to an undifferentiated mass such as 'sky'. An abstract noun is something you can't see or touch such as 'fear' or 'loneliness' or 'silence'.

We have already noticed how odd it sounds to repeat a noun over and over again in a text. In the story about Sam, it would have sounded more natural to replace the name after the first time, with 'he'. This is an example of a class of words called 'pronouns', which, as the name suggests, can work 'on behalf of' nouns. Very often, the ones that stand in as a subject or object of a sentence belong to a subgroup called personal pronouns. They are used more frequently than any other types of pronoun.

Adjectives

Adjectives are a powerful word class provided they are used with discretion. On page 10 we mentioned the 'dark, dark wood' (from Ruth Brown's dramatic picture book *A Dark, Dark Tale*). In this example, the adjective 'dark' is telling us more about the noun 'wood', and its effect is heightened by the repetition. Adjectives can give us more information about:

- Numbers or amounts of things: two, hundreds, loads.
- The colour of things: green, striped, mud-coloured.
- The feel: soft, furrowed, scratchy.

Sometimes they can become tired and overworked. We've probably all winced in the motorway café when we've been offered 'dew-fresh mushrooms' which are actually nothing of the kind. Encourage the children, when you are sharing books with them, to find and enjoy powerful, exciting, humorous and innovative adjectives (there are four for you in a row!).

Verbs

Verbs are a very large and complex word class and it would probably not help you to try to summarise all that could be said about them in a few sentences. Of all the words in a sentence, the nouns and the verbs are the most vital parts: they are the words that are crucial for the sentence to make sense. The nouns tell us who or what is being talked about, and the verbs tell us what's happening to those named people or things or what the state of them is. It would be useful to try to explore at least these aspects of verbs: person, tense, mood and voice.

Person

Writers can choose to structure their texts in the first person:

I am going to tell you what happened to me in Paris.

Or they can opt for the more impersonal third person:

Water is one of our most precious commodities.

John Kennedy was a famous American president.

Sometimes, writers can choose to address their readers directly using the second person:

You will find it hard to believe the story I am about to tell you.

What matters, when you are sharing a book with children, is not spotting whether the text is written in the first, second or third person, but thinking about the effect the choice has on the readers.

Tense

A writer must decide whether the text is to be in one of the forms of the present or in a past tense. English has no future tense ending but it has several ways of expressing future time. Usually, once they have chosen a past or present tense, writers retain that tense throughout. It might be interesting to look for any changes and talk about why they have occurred. Direct speech, for example, might necessitate a change to the present tense.

Mood

There are three possible 'moods': indicative, interrogative and imperative. You are not likely to be using any of these technical terms with the children, but as you already know (implicitly), asking questions (interrogative mood) or giving commands (imperative mood) does necessitate some restructuring of grammar from merely making statements (indicative mood). We have already mentioned that at certain times you will want to draw children's attention to the way writers have handled these grammatical choices.

Active and passive voice

Consider this sentence.

David Beckham scored the goal.

If you have persisted with reading this chapter so far, you will recognise the pattern of this sentence:

subject	verb	object
David Beckham	scored	the goal.

The emphasis here is placed on the famous player – he did the scoring. This is an active sentence. Suppose, however, that the writer of the newspaper article wanted to highlight the goal, rather than the player. The sentence can be turned round:

The goal was scored by David Beckham.

This time the subject of the sentence is the goal. Of course it did not 'score itself' – David Beckham is the 'agent' but he is relegated to a slightly less prominent place in the sentence. It would be possible for a journalist, irritated by all the coverage given to David Beckham, to decide not to mention him at all and to write:

A goal was scored.

Sometimes, in controversial cases, it's quite useful to be able to avoid mentioning who was responsible for the action.

Adverbs

Again these have been mentioned already. Readers of the above newspaper article might like to know:

- When the goal was scored (in the first few seconds).
- How (in a thrilling run down the field).
- Why (because the defence had taken their eyes off the ball).
- Where (in the penalty area).

Words that provide these kinds of information about the action (in this case scoring) are known as adverbs. You may notice that sometimes one word is used or sometimes a group of words, known as a phrase or a clause. If the teacher asks you to do some work on any of these you can find more information in the sources listed at the end of the chapter.

Summary

In this chapter we have discussed:

- Knowledge about syntax that helps us to read.
- A definition of a sentence.
- Sentence connectives.
- Word classes.

Further reading

DfEE (2001) *National Literacy Strategy Framework for Teaching.* London: DfEE.

Thomson, R. (2002) *Focus on Writing: Go Further with Grammar.* London: Belitha Press.

Wilson, A. (2001) *Language Knowledge for Primary Teachers.* London: David Fulton Publishers (esp. Chs 6 and 7).

Wray, D. and Medwell, J. (2001) *Teaching English in Primary Schools* (2nd edn). London: Letts.

Chapter 5

Reading in the Foundation Stage and Key Stage 1

This and the following two chapters will examine the way reading is approached in school by focusing on a variety of texts, activities and resources that can be used to support children in the classroom.

How is reading taught in the primary classroom?

This is a very important question. In the first chapter we described a scenario, familiar to us all, where children were called to the teacher who *listened* to them read on an individual basis (Julie was allowed a sherbet pip from a Tartan Shortbread tin if she read all of her words correctly!). Although this type of reading (without the sugary reward) may still take place in school, it is often considered an additional reading activity to offer support rather than the only method of *teaching* reading.

The words *listened* and *teaching* are vital to understanding how the approach to reading has changed. The advent of the National Curriculum and the National Literacy Strategy has firmly placed the emphasis on teaching reading strategies rather than listening to children read. Therefore, in order to provide the teacher with more opportunity to spend time directly teaching the children in his/her class, the government recommended a shift in the balance of teaching from 'individualised work...towards more whole class and group teaching' (DfEE 1998: 10). The process of whole-class teaching was intended to be, and remains, an interactive one, with the teacher and children working together using a wide range of resources. You will undoubtedly have come across them if you have spent any time in school: big books and stands, magnetic whiteboards and letters, small whiteboards, phonic wheels and slides, over-head projectors, interactive whiteboards etc. Big books are now a feature in classrooms – most are commercially produced but some are made by school staff and children. Whatever book is used in your classroom for shared reading, ensure that the children at the back can see the words on the page. Overhead projectors and interactive whiteboards are in schools and can be used as presentational tools, but in the early years of school, the handling of a book needs to be modelled for the children by the teacher and teaching assistant. Therefore the use of presentational technologies in both Reception and Key Stage 1 classrooms has to be carefully considered. We will look at specific examples of other resources later in this and the following two chapters.

Shared reading

This whole-class part of the lesson is known as the **shared** section of the literacy lesson. Of course, we will focus on shared reading in this book (information on shared writing activities can be found in *Supporting Writing* in this series). Shared reading is usually teacher-led but we have spoken to teaching assistants who have been asked to conduct this part of a lesson with a whole class, or a year group when working in a mixed year group class. In any case, the role of the teaching assistant is vital in these sessions and involves working closely with the teacher:

● Echoing points made by the teacher or in some cases refining or rephrasing them to help children who are slow to respond.

● Working with the teacher, for example in the use of puppets or demon-strating how to use a dictionary.

● Pointing out children who have not contributed or who appear to be struggling.

The Department for Education and Skills (DfES) has more guidance on the role of teaching assistants in the shared section of the literacy hour on its website (www.standards.dfes.gov.uk). At Key Stage 1, there is a focus on word level work during much of the period of whole-class teaching.

Guided reading

Following the shared section of the literacy hour, the teacher will go on to do some focused work with a small group of children of similar ability: this is known as **guided** reading. As a teaching assistant, the teacher may ask you to work with a guided reading group. For example, you may read a poem and encourage the children to locate and list any rhyming words.

A world of words

In addition to formal lessons, young children need to be surrounded by words. In the Foundation Stage children must be able to make the link between and become aware of the differences in spoken and written language. For example:

- It is important to provide a quiet 'language area' where children can read and have stories read and told to them.

- A listening post where children can listen to a story while following the story in the book is also useful as the child develops book-handling skills (turning pages at a beep) and listening skills, which help with sound recognition.

- Labelling trays etc. with children's names is also key to the link between spoken and written language. In Julie's school, the nursery teacher has made named placemats for use at breaktime and has also labelled chairs.

- Another school registers their children by the use of name cards. The children come into school, find their name card and drop it into a basket.

- Names are often a great source of inspiration for reading activities – children love to spot the letters from their own and their friends' names. A four-year-old, terribly excited after reading the word Friday, shouted 'F... like Fleur!' (Fleur being her friend). It is amazing to see how the children relate to the sound/letter correspondence in each other's names.

- The day, month, date and weather conditions can also be displayed; the children will soon become familiar with reading days of the week etc. Julie's Year 1 class has a weather board containing all of this information which is updated daily – the children love to chant the new information.

Phonics in the Foundation Stage and Key Stage 1

As we have said previously, there is a focus on word level work for Reception and Key Stage 1 children. Government guidelines state that as part of this word level work, 'phonics should be the main focus' (DfEE/QCA 2000: 7). Indeed, it goes further, recommending the systematic teaching of phonics in isolation away from texts, although it is possible to use a word from a text as a springboard into the particular phonics focus, for example a Year 2 class in Term 2 may read the traditional tale *Chicken Licken* for words containing the digraph 'ch' (DfEE 1998: 22). The reasoning behind this is that providing children with an understanding of phonics will help them both to decode words and to spell words by being able to recognise them by their common spelling patterns (see *Supporting Spelling* in this series). Therefore, when you are in school working with a Reception or Key Stage 1 class, you will see a great emphasis on developing a phonemic awareness. It will be interesting for you to consider how this work is taught in conjunction with text and sentence level objectives. It is always more relevant to the children if there is a link between the three strands of word, sentence and text level.

A shared reading session in a Reception class

One school's Reception class recently demonstrated how to integrate the daily phonics focus with text and sentence level work. All three aspects were generated from a 'sound of the week' which was linked to the 'big book of the week' and to a 'silly sentences of the week'. The teaching assistant and teacher worked closely together in all aspects of the literacy hour.

One particular week, the sound was 't', the big book was *Where's My Teddy?* by Jez Alborough and a new word for sentence work was 'toy'. The week began with a phonics focus: the children all brought an object, the name of which began with the sound 't' ('identify initial phonemes', DfEE 1998: 18). One little boy brought a truck. The teaching assistant took the truck and passed it to the teacher, who asked her the questions 'Does this begin with our sound?' and 'What is it?' The teaching assistant shook her head: 'It can't go on the table, it's a lorry', she said feigning disappointment. It was a fantastic double act and the children took great delight in telling the adults they were wrong by shouting out 'It's a truck!' with emphasis on the 't' of course. This gathering-in process took quite a while but made an eye-catching weekly display of relevant objects. When all the objects had been collected together, the children swivelled around 45 degrees to turn to face an empty big book stand. The big book was slowly revealed to them and text level reading objectives became the focus.

The first day with a book involved the children focusing on the cover and title page to meet the Reception year text level objective 'to understand and correctly use terms about books' (DfEE 1998: 18). It is important to remember that children arrive at school with varying degrees of knowledge about language and books. Some will have been immersed in books from a very early age while others may never have handled a book. Therefore these early sessions involve modelling reading behaviours. In this case, the children were shown:

- How to look at the book the right way up.
- The features of the front cover – title, author and illustrator.
- How to track the text in the right direction, the teacher using her finger to familiarise the children with reading from left to right.

The picture was discussed to discover what the children thought the book was going to be about, as was the purpose of the blurb on the back cover. Other markings on the book should also be pointed out, e.g. ISBN numbers, publisher details and bar codes. Discuss with the children why they are there. Opening the book brought an interesting comment from one child who said 'That doesn't belong to you! It is from the library, I get books with those tickets in!' This comment provided the teacher with an insight into the child's experience of books.

The actual story was left until the following day. Then only the first half was read and the book was left open on the stand for the children to study so that they could make a prediction as to what was going to happen next in the book. It was finished on the third day and revisited for the remaining two days to focus on sentence and word level objectives. We feel that this approach of taking time with a text, leaving the children wanting more and then revisiting it, is invaluable to successful literacy teaching – especially reading because as the children become more familiar with the text they are more able to identify language features and join in the reading process.

The sentence level work was based on simple high frequency words: 'the', 'and', 'went' etc. plus CVC words (consonant/vowel/consonant). Silly sentences were made up using pre-printed words on sentence rods. The children read them as a class and made suggestions as to why they were wrong. For example: 'The bus went on the dog.' Again they pointed out enthusiastically that a bus would squash a dog and suggested that the dog and bus should be swapped about. Similar sentences were constructed introducing the new word 'toy'.

This example of a 'shared' section of a literacy hour shows how careful planning can result in a more integrated approach to phonics teaching. The text was chosen to support the word level objectives of that particular week, providing the children with opportunities to see the phoneme/grapheme correspondence in print, in a story they enjoyed. Therefore it is important that you familiarise yourself with a range of children's books as it will enable you, if asked by the teacher, to choose a text to read with children which will build on their word level skills and develop their confidence. For example, Year 1 Term 2 has a word level learning objective to read and spell words ending in 'ck'. You may choose the story *Farmer Duck* by Martin Waddell as the story has a range of such words: 'duck', 'quack', 'cluck', 'back' etc. The book also has a patterned text with lots of repeated words and phrases and is therefore appropriate for beginner readers.

Phonics/word level activities

Following a whole-class shared reading session, the children will move on to group or individual activities with a word level focus. Some activities may also be suitable for whole-class teaching with children working as individuals or in pairs.

Foundation Stage

Activities may include:

- Making a specific letter and an object beginning with that letter's sound using plasticine.

- Drawing letters in wet sand.
- Tray game – each child is given an object and they have to choose an object from a tray that has the same initial phoneme.
- Using letter fans to show what letter represents the phoneme in a given position in a word, e.g. initial, medial, final phoneme, depending on the age and ability of the child.
- Using magnetic letters to read and spell simple words. One child recently said it was easier to read and write with magnetic letters not only because he could feel their shape but also because they were colourful, easy to see and it was 'tricky' to write with a pen. They can be a great asset to building enthusiasm for reading.
- Using phonic slides to spell words by changing initial letter only (see diagram below).

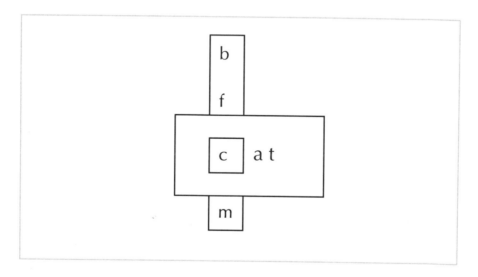

(These slides are easy to make using A4 card. A strip of card is fed through the A4 sheet to show a changing initial letter. Make one and try it with the children in school.)

Key Stage 1

You can develop activities to include letter blends, digraphs etc. (see Chapter 2). Some examples are:

- Noisy letters – the children are given a card containing a letter or digraph, e.g. 'sh'. They make their given sound and team up with other children making the same sound.
- Sound bingo – make some letter/digraph bingo cards. You say a word – if a child has the initial/medial/final sound (depending on age and ability) on their card they cover it up.
- Phonic slides/wheels – similar to the slides previously discussed but they will include final phonemes, blends, digraphs etc.

The teacher may ask you to either support specific children or lead one of these activities: this will provide you with an opportunity to observe the children and talk to them in order to judge their understanding. You may ask questions such as:

- How did you make that?
- What did you find easy/difficult?
- What object have you chosen to make? Why?
- How did you know to choose that letter?
- What sound did you hear at the beginning/middle/end of that word?

Your findings can be fed back to the teacher to help with assessment and progression.

Although we have focused on phonics, it is important to understand that children need to be taught other skills, as set out in the searchlights model (on p. 14) to make them effective and competent readers. They need to experience a range of text types and even in these early years begin to understand their particular features and purpose. Picture books are a fantastic tool both for introducing the process of reading and for building enthusiasm even at Key Stage 2 (more on that in the following chapter). The children should begin to respond to texts by offering thoughts and opinions. We will now go on to consider the use of narrative (story), poetry and non-fiction texts.

I Don't Want to Go to Bed! Julia Sykes

What type of text is this?

This is a story. It tells the tale of a young tiger who doesn't want to go to bed. He wants to play with his friends in the jungle. Mum gets fed up and lets him stay up. In turn he visits his friends who are all in bed. Suddenly it is dark and Tiger is tired and afraid until a bushbaby leads him home.

The illustrations are colourful and interesting, and offer opportunity for lots of discussion. At the text level it provides opportunities to discuss a number of issues and feelings that will be familiar to the children: bedtime routines, not wanting to go to bed, fear of the dark, loneliness, making new friends etc. If you are sharing this book, discuss these feelings. Ask the children questions:

- How is Tiger feeling at the beginning/end of the book?
- Why have his feelings changed?
- When have you ever not wanted to go to bed?
- Why was the bushbaby awake?
- How was Tiger feeling when he met the bushbaby? Have you ever felt like that?

Don't forget to point out all the features of the book: title, author, illustrator, blurb, ISBN, bar code and publisher and discuss their roles. Also remember to track the text with your finger.

Sentences and words

The book contains a lot of patterned language. The sentences 'It's bedtime', 'Why are you still up?' and 'I don't want to go to bed!' are repeated throughout the book, allowing the children to predict what will follow and join in the reading. You will often see the teacher covering up a word in such a sentence so that the children can make their predictions, after which the word is slowly revealed. Alternatively, a puppet may read the wrong words only to be corrected by the children. The use of bold type, the reasons for this and how such words are read should be discussed. You should also highlight punctuation, especially the use of question and exclamation marks if this text is being used at Years 1 and 2. The author has used some descriptive vocabulary including alliteration ('big, bright') to describe the bushbaby's eyes.

Activities with this text

The following activities are suggestions that support the National Literacy Strategy objectives (Reception–Year 2). You may be asked to work with children carrying out similar activities when you are in school. All involve the children reading and demonstrating an understanding of the text, although some may be writing or drama (speaking and listening) activities.

- The children could write their own sentence 'I don't want to go to bed because...' When Julie carried out this activity with a Year 1 class (Term 2 Text Level Objective 13 – 'to substitute and extend patterns from reading'), one little girl completed the sentence by writing 'because I could not find my pyjamas!'

- Children have lots of fun generating alliterations and you may be asked to work with them to generate more in order to describe other characters from the text.

- Order the main points of the story in the correct sequence. This may be done as a story board.

- The author's use of interesting verbs to describe Tiger's movement – 'skipped', 'bounced', 'scurried' and 'tiptoed' – could be used in a group dramatisation of the story.

Traditional stories

What are traditional stories?

In Key Stage 1, traditional stories are traditional folk and fairy tales which also include stories from other cultures, for example *Cinderella* (French), *Jack and the Beanstalk* (English), *The Snake Prince* (Indian) etc. (*Myths and Fairy Tales Collection* by Neil Philip is an invaluable book that not only retells stories from around the world but offers factual background information, see 'Further reading' at the end of this chapter.) Children will probably be familiar with many such stories, if not through books through pantomimes or the delights of Disney! Therefore they present a good starting point for reading in that they are not only familiar but they also have a range of features peculiar to this genre, from the 'Once upon a time' (or similar) opening to the 'Happy ever after' ending.

The Enormous Watermelon Brenda Parkes and Judith Smith

What type of text is this?

It is a simple traditional tale about a man and woman who plant a watermelon that grows to be so enormous they have to summon help to pull it from the ground. Children may be familiar with this story as an enormous turnip and may draw on this knowledge. This link to another text is known as 'intertextuality' and applying this knowledge can be a real help to beginner readers as the familiarity helps them to tackle the text more confidently. This particular story is full of intertextual links as the two main characters call on a range of familiar nursery rhyme characters to help them to pull up the watermelon: Humpty Dumpty, Wee Willie Winkie, Jack and Jill etc. The children can use picture clues, discreetly positioned in the bottom right-hand corner of the page, to help them predict which character will appear next. When you are sharing this book with a group of children ask them how they know who is coming next – they really are quick to spot the clues and apply their knowledge of nursery rhyme characters. This book was 'shared' with groups of undergraduates training to be primary teachers who failed to spot the picture clues until halfway through the book! We can only assume that, in order to make sense of the text, young children in a Reception class will study the pictures in more detail while adults focus on the written text. The story ends with the characters all tucking into a piece of the watermelon. Discuss alternative endings with the children.

Sentences and words

The text is heavily patterned with a lot of repetition of sentences and words. In addition to repeated phrases, e.g. 'They pulled and they pulled and they pulled', are the characters' names which appear each time there is an attempt to pull up the watermelon. There is also use of bold type and capitalisation for emphasis when reading.

Activities with this text

The following activities are suggestions that support the National Literacy Strategy objectives for Reception and Year 1 Term 1:

- Dramatise the story. Give each child or pair a character name card for them to read. Then work with them to sequence the characters/story in the correct order and act out the story.
- Sequence the events of the story using a range of pictures from the text.
- Re-enact/retell the story using the names of the children in the class in alphabetical order. This takes a lot of organisation and you and the teacher will have to work closely together. You may be asked to make a life-sized display by drawing around each child. The silhouettes could then be coloured, name-labelled by the children concerned and displayed in the alphabetical order of the class re-enactment. Good luck!
- Make a simple storybook using the patterned text as a model. Encourage the children to use a different fruit/vegetable and a smaller selection of nursery rhyme characters of their choice.

Poetry

The Sunshine Tree

If I had just one wish to wish
Do you know what it would be?
That growing in my garden
Was a great big sunshine tree.

A tree that never rained or blew
A tree that shone all day.
And there I'd sit with all my toys
And play and play and play.

Clive Webster

What type of text is it?

This is a short poem which describes the poet's one wish – to have a sunshine tree. We know that it is a poem because it has a rhythm when you read it and in this case it rhymes (every second line). There are two verses or stanzas. At text level, the children should be encouraged to look at the shape and organisation of the poem, as well as what they think it is about. Julie recently used this poem with her Year 1 class (Term 3: 24 'read a variety of poems on similar themes'), who made some really interesting comments. She approached the shared reading by only displaying the title and first two lines of the poem. This allowed the children to discuss what the poet's wish might be. A number guessed correctly by referring back to the title. The class then discussed the author's feelings at the time he wrote the poem and also when it might have been written. One boy was confident that the poet had written it in the winter when it was raining: 'He was probably bored and wanted to play out, that's how I feel when it rains' he commented. But a girl, who struggles to decode, put up her hand and whispered, 'I think the poet is like me, afraid of the dark, because if the tree was outside his bedroom it would always be light and he would never be afraid again.' The girl, who had agreed with the comments by the boy, was taking her understanding of the poem a step further and relating it to her own life. Although she was not able to read all the words, she was showing an excellent understanding, which is a significant part of the reading process.

Words and punctuation

The language is simple and includes a number of high frequency words and so can be read by the majority of Year 1 children. The word 'sunshine' is a compound word and the more able in the class were immediately able to break it down into its two parts: sun-shine. The others used a phonetic strategy for the first part of the word and 'guessed' the rest. This shows the children beginning to use a range of strategies including contextual clues. There are two sets of rhyming words in the poem – be/tree and day/play. The only description of the tree comes from 'great', 'big' and 'sunshine'. Repetition of the words, 'wish' and 'play' add emphasis to the poet's main points within the poem.

The punctuation is typical of a traditional poem, i.e. a capital letter to begin each new line. The poem begins with a question allowing discussion of the question mark, its position and purpose.

Activities with this text

Some activities which support the reading of the text would be:

- A guided writing activity suggesting why the children would like a sunshine tree in their garden.
- A guided or independent writing activity to create a verse of a poem by substituting a sunshine tree with their own wish.
- To draw or make their own wish tree and write a title.
- To list a set of rhyming words based on the rhymes within the poem.
- To investigate more compound words (Year 2 Term 2)
- To generate other CVC words to rhyme with 'big' (Reception)

Non-fiction

Discovery World: My Body Rhonda Jenkins

What type of text is this?

This is a very simple non-chronological report which offers information about the body as the title suggests! It is visually stimulating from the photograph of the little girl wearing a fluorescent pink and black spotted swimming costume, pink goggles and armbands on the front cover, to the photographs of other children (girls and boys) who all introduce a particular part of their own body, which is accompanied by a labelled diagram and mock X-ray to show the bone formation.

When sharing a non-fiction text, continue to point out all the relevant 'book' features on the cover but pay special attention to the back cover where the blurb may be organised differently. In this case, information about the book is provided using a series of bullet points (actually a list from the contents page). The children will focus on the bullet points and be able to transfer some of the knowledge to the contents page. The contents page is vital in the use of a non-fiction text. You must emphasise that an information book is different from a story because it does not have to be read from cover to cover. Instead the reader chooses the part he wants to read. Discuss the purpose and position of the **contents page** – at the beginning of the book, providing a list of what is included in the book (in order of appearance) to help you locate the information you need. This must be distinguished from the **index** which is found at the back of the book and is in alphabetical order. Go on to ask the children questions such as:

- What are we going to find out about today? They may suggest 'the leg and foot'.
- How can we find the page that has information about the leg and foot?
- What page is it on? How did you know?
- What else could we use to find information about the foot?
- How is the index page different from the contents page?

This particular book has a useful, graphic index page: each subject has a supporting drawing, allowing the children to draw on a range of strategies to read the page. The labelled diagrams play an important part in this text. Discuss with the children the features of labelled diagrams and how they work – the carefully drawn line to the relevant body part, the clear single-word labels. Find out what the children think about the diagrams. Have the labels helped them to understand the book? Would the book have been as interesting without them?

Sentences and words

Each subject covers a double-page spread. The left-hand page repeats the first part of a sentence, 'This is my...', providing a patterned structure. The sentence is completed by whatever part of the body is being explained, e.g. 'This is my head', 'This is my chest' etc. A child is pictured above the sentence, pointing to the said body part. Again this allows the reader to use picture clues to tackle any unknown words. The right-hand page is devoted to the labelled diagram. The vocabulary is very general. For example, the head has the following labels: nose, eye, mouth and ear. Some vocabulary is more difficult, e.g. shoulder. The children should be encouraged to use the picture clues to read these less familiar words.

Activities with this text

The book lends itself particularly well to Year 1 Term 2. Some activities which support the reading of the text are:

- To produce a labelled diagram of their own body parts as part of a guided writing activity.
- To make a book based on the text, about themselves or a pet, e.g. 'My Dog', using simple sentences and labelled diagrams.
- To use the word 'hand' to begin an investigation into words ending in 'nd'.
- To use the word 'neck' to begin an investigation into words ending in 'ck'.
- Play a game, locating information using the contents or index page. Use small whiteboards for the children to write their responses to your questions, e.g. On what page will I find out about the head?
- A guided reading activity to compare the cover and layout of another text to the shared text.

Summary

In this chapter we have discussed:

- How reading is taught in the primary classroom and the move away from individual to whole-class teaching.
- The teaching of phonics; its place in the literacy hour and some ideas for activities which may be carried out with the children.
- Specific examples of a range of texts at text, sentence and word level and ideas for activities in the classroom.

Further reading

Brown, A. (1996) *Developing Language and Literacy 3–8*. London: Paul Chapman Publishing.

Clipson-Boyles, S. (2001) *Supporting Language and Literacy 3–8*. London: David Fulton Publishers.

DfEE (1998) *National Literacy Strategy Framework for Teaching*. London: DfEE.

DfEE/QCA (2000) *Curriculum Guidance for the Foundation Stage*. London: DfEE/QCA.

Foster, J. (1993) *Twinkle, Twinkle Chocolate Bar: Rhymes for the Very Young*. Oxford: OUP.

Jenkins, Rhonda (1999) *Discovery World: My Body*. London: Heinemann.

Merchant, G. and Thomas, H. (1999) *Picture Books for the Literacy Hour*. London: David Fulton Publishers.

Parkes, Brenda and Smith, Judith (1997) *The Enormous Watermelon*. Bothell, WA: Mimosa Publications.

Philip, N. (1999) *Myths and Fairy Tales Collection*. London: Dorling Kindersley.

Sykes, Julia (1997) *I Don't Want to Go to Bed!* Illustrated by Tim Warnes. London: Little Tiger Press.

Chapter 6

Reading in Key Stage 2: book texts

This and the following chapter will examine how reading can be developed during Key Stage 2 in order for children to reach the expected Level 4 Attainment Target, as set out in the National Curriculum, by the end of Year 6. This chapter will focus on book texts and aims to make you more aware of the characteristics of each text type. It will include examples of fiction, poetry and non-fiction texts along with ideas for activities in the classroom.

How is reading different at Key Stage 2?

By the time children enter Key Stage 2 they are expected to be able to:

● Read simple texts showing an understanding and with accuracy.

● Express opinions about major events or ideas in texts.

● Use more than one strategy to read and understand unfamiliar words.

If the children have not reached Level 2 as they enter Year 3, you may be asked to carry out focused reading activities with them as part of the Additional Literacy Support programme. Activities will usually be phonics-based and similar to those described in the previous chapter.

The fact that children are expected to have mastered the initial skills of reading during Key Stage 1 means that at Key Stage 2 emphasis is placed on interacting with, and responding to, a wider range of more demanding texts, with the aim of developing critical reading skills. It is important to motivate those children who feel they have learnt enough to be able to read what they want to read and so don't have to do any more work. In order to achieve the expected Level 4 at the end of Year 6, children should be able to:

- Infer and deduce meanings.
- Show an understanding of ideas, themes, events and characters.
- Express their views and refer to the text to support their views.
- Classify the type of text.
- Locate and use information.

Teaching strategies and resources

Both shared and guided reading remain the two main teaching strategies during focused literacy lessons (see previous chapter). However, you may notice a significant difference in how texts are presented for whole-class teaching with less emphasis on word level work.

Presentational technologies such as the interactive whiteboard and over-head projector are used much more frequently as these allow the teacher and children to highlight and manipulate a piece of text more easily. Julie will never forget observing a Year 6 class using an interactive whiteboard to study a Shakespeare play! The children read a scene from *A Midsummer Night's Dream* and went on to identify Shakespearian adjectives and then to suggest modern-day equivalents. The children were mesmerised by the whiteboard and were very keen to highlight the adjectives and then delete them and insert their own suggestions.

Text marking and note-making are strategies used by the teacher and children (see pp. 82 and 89) to draw attention to specific features and words in a text. The teacher may highlight the words 'title', 'ingredients' and 'method' when using a recipe as an example of an instructional text. After discussion with the class, the teacher and a selection of children may go on to write in the margin the various points that were discussed, for example the purpose of each area of the text and specific language features. Other activities used to develop reading are:

- Class readers – a class will read a book for half a term to a term. Usually the children take it in turns to read. Some may feel daunted by this, so be aware and report any problems to the teacher.
- Literary circles – a group of children may review a book or discuss their favourite books. They should be encouraged to give specific reasons for their opinions by referring specifically to the text.

- Paired reading – children share books with a regular reading partner. This may be a child in the same class or a less able or more able child. Julie's Year 5 children have been taking part in a scheme to read in pairs to a group of Reception or Year 1 children. They chose an appropriate book and were given time to read through and rehearse their reading. It gave them a real understanding of the structure of young children's books and also confidence in reading aloud. One girl announced 'I think they would like this one because it has lots of the same word they can join in with.'

- Reading journals/diaries – children may be asked to keep a diary of all they read. They will probably have to note what they read, its purpose and target audience and what it was about. They may also be asked to state whether or not they liked it and why. Encourage them to include everything they read. One teacher told her Year 3 class to include instructions for computer games, shopping lists and even Safeway flyers! This type of activity really does make the children aware of the need to be able to read for a range of purposes. They may also keep a diary of book reviews. These will have a different format which will depend upon the age and reading ability of the children.

- Silent reading – children reading their chosen book silently for enjoyment is still a feature of many Key Stage 2 classrooms. However, many schools will demand that the children have a reading focus during this time, for example a character in a story.

Narrative/story texts

This is a vast area to cover but we will look at some general features of such texts that allow the reader to make meaning before looking at two examples.

Narrative texts at Key Stage 2 become longer and more complex as the children progress through the key stage. 'So they should!' you may say. But this can result in difficulties for the teacher who is trying to include a wide range of text types in order to meet the learning objectives set out in the National Literacy Strategy. What you will probably see if you are working in Key Stage 2 is the use of extracts from storybooks. Although understandable, this is far from ideal as the children are unable to see how a story unfolds, how the characters are developed and the effect of the setting. You may work in a school that tries to overcome this problem by having a class 'novel for the term' which is read daily to the children, and extracts of which are used as a focus for literacy teaching. It may be your responsibility to read such a book with the class. If this is the case, take a copy home and familiarise yourself with the story before sharing it with the class. This will help you to identify the main themes, crucial points in the plot and features of character development, which in turn will enable you to 'lay down the foundations of how, as readers, we make contact with the world of the book' (Reid and Bentley 1996: 11).

Features of narrative texts

There is a wide range of narrative texts that should be studied at Key Stage 2: traditional stories (including fables, myths, legends etc.), short novels, classic fiction and stories from other cultures to name but a few! In all cases you will need to be aware of how a story works. The elements of a story can be broken down into three main parts:

- Plot – the story structure and what happens. When working on plot with the children encourage them not only to predict what may happen, but also to consider the link between events and how often one event *causes* another to happen.

- Character – the people, animals etc. Think about character being developed by the author through **dialogue** (what and how something is said), **description** (how the character looks, sounds and smells), and **actions** and **attitudes** (what the character does and the response of other characters). The children should be encouraged to select specific words and phrases to support their opinion of a character.

- Setting – where the action takes place. Look out for descriptive words and phrases. Find out what the children think about a setting. Ask questions such as: How does it make you feel? Where have you been that might be like that? What do you like/dislike about it? Again they should refer to specific words from the text to support their views.

Story openings

Story openings should grab the reader's attention and make them want to read on. In the previous chapter you found out how to identify a traditional story by its opening sentence. Contemporary fiction tends to begin in one of three ways, by:

● introducing a character;
● describing a setting;
● dialogue between characters.

Activity

You may be asked to support a group while they read a selection of openings. Encourage the children to look for similarities between the texts, to discuss their preferred openings and to give reasons and to make a decision as to which book they would go on to read and why. They could then present their findings to the rest of the class. Julie carried out this activity with a group of Year 5 children and what was interesting was that they dismissed the traditional Grimm's fairy tale with the comment 'Stories that begin with 'Once...' are for babies, we did them in the infants!' However, they were keen to read *Bill's New Frock* by Anne Fine as they wanted to find out if the character, Bill, who had been introduced in the opening, was a girl or a boy. This particular opening prompted some interesting discussion about the role of parents and how the children felt about themselves. The children really were responding to the issues introduced at the beginning of the text and showing a good understanding of what they had read.

The Lion and the Mouse

What type of text is this?

This is a fable (you are probably familiar with a number of Aesop's fables including *The Tortoise and the Hare, The Raven and the Fox* etc.), i.e. a short story with a moral. It tells the story of a lion which trapped a mouse under its paw. Instead of killing the mouse, the lion released it. In turn, the mouse gnawed through a hunter's net to release the captured lion, despite the lion thinking that the mouse was too small to help.

Typical features of this and other fables are:

- **Title** – this usually consists of the names of the characters in the story.
- **Opening** – traditional story openings are used, for example, 'One fine day...', 'Once...', 'One day...' etc.
- **Characters** – the characters are almost always animals that have anthropomorphic qualities, i.e. they take on human characteristics and can, therefore, talk, have feelings etc.
- **Moral** – perhaps the most identifiable feature of a fable is its moral or lesson. The moral for *The Lion and the Mouse* is that small friends can be powerful friends.

Activities

You may be asked to carry out a number of reading activities which would support the learning objectives for Year 3 Term 2 and Year 5 Term 2.

- Text marking – read through a selection of fables and encourage the children to highlight the features previously identified. Ask the children questions to establish that they have identified similarities between the texts, for example: What do you notice about all of the characters? How do the fables begin? etc.
- Devise morals – in preparation for writing a full fable, you may have to work with children who are devising their own moral. This can be daunting for children who are not familiar with fables so encourage them to identify the main points in the story and how the characters may feel at those points and at the end. Julie carried out this activity in a mixed Year 2/3 class and one of the younger children was able to provide a moral to every fable. She was amazed until he told her that he listened to an audio tape of Aesop's fables every day in the car! At least he had remembered them and the activity made him brim with confidence.
- Fable cards – these are a good method of encouraging children to write a fable. It is 'fables by Cluedo!' Three sets of cards are produced: the first

set has the name of an animal written on each card (e.g. elephant, worm, mouse etc.); the second set has a setting written on each card (e.g. in a mountain village, on the farm, beneath a tree etc.); the third set has a moral written on each card (e.g. *slow and steady wins the race*). Each child takes two character and one each of the setting and moral cards. They can use the information to write their own fable.

Conker **Michael Morpurgo**

What type of text is it?

This is an example of contemporary fiction. It tells the story of a boy, Nick, who lives with his grandmother. He is being bullied by a boy at school but has a friend in his grandmother's Alsatian dog, Old Station, who dies in the first chapter of the story. His grandmother puts all her efforts into helping him create a championship conker to enable him to beat his bully in a conker championship. Meanwhile Nick discovers a maltreated guard dog during his search for conkers and plots to rescue him. It has a happy ending as his grandmother takes ownership of the dog unbeknown to Nick, who thinks he has been destroyed by the vet. Incidentally, Nick wins his conker tournament too and so names his new dog Conker!

It is a story that contains a number of poignant but relevant themes such as bereavement, bullying, abuse and love. A group of Year 5 children commented that it was a great story because it was real 'Like things that happen to us.' If you share this book (or similar books) with the children in your class, discuss:

- The relationships between the characters.
- The characters' different reactions to the different events.
- Similar events that have happened in their own lives and their feelings.

Sentences and words

An interesting feature is that the first three words of every chapter are in bold type to highlight a new beginning. There is quite a lot of conversation in the text which allows you to discuss how the dialogue is punctuated and also how the author uses adverbs such as 'quietly' and 'quickly' to qualify the dialogue, e.g. '"Your turn," Nick said quietly as he held up his conker.' There are details of Grandma's recipe for conker potion and a picture listing the ingredients. The recipe is not presented in true instructional form and you should ask the children to think about why the author has not simply included a recipe. The author uses a number of descriptive words and phrases, for example 'bragging, brutish boy'. This is an example of alliteration (each word begins with the same sound), and emphasises the image of the bully, Stevie Rooster. The name Rooster lends itself to some investigation. The children should be encouraged to think about the significance of this name and make links between rooster, cock, cocky etc.

Activities

The following activities support the National Literacy Strategy learning objectives for Year 4 Term 3 and Year 5 Term 1.

- Alternative ending – ask the children to consider other ways the book may have ended. These may include Nick rescuing the dog, the vet destroying the dog etc. Encourage the children to be realistic and base their ideas on and make close links with what they have read. They can then write their alternative ending.

- Identifying character – word process a passage from the text that describes a character, for example Stevie Rooster the bully. Ask the children to underline the words that tell you something about the character. Then the children can rewrite the passage, changing those words to make Stevie a pleasant character. Julie once carried out this activity using the aunts from *James and the Giant Peach* by Roald Dahl. The following day a boy rushed up to her and said 'You won't believe it but authors describe places as well!' He went on to share a description of Diagon Alley from J.K. Rowling's *Harry Potter and the Philosopher's Stone* that he had read the previous evening – a promising response from a reluctant reader.

- Character portraits – encourage the children to select their favourite character from the book. Discuss what they like about them and how they know what they are like by referring to specific parts of the text. The children can structure their information and write a character portrait.

● Drama – choose a scene from the text and work with the children to enact it. The conker championship in this book would be ideal and would also support the PSHE (personal, social and health education) curriculum.

● Hot seating – this is a good way of exploring character. A child takes on the role of a character in the book and others in the group ask questions based on the text. For example, if a child was in the role of Nick, others in the group may ask questions such as 'How did you feel when your dog died?' and 'Why did you throw Stevie's conker into the pond?' Encourage the children to work together to formulate their questions in order to avoid repetition.

Poetry

'The Highwayman' by Alfred Noyes

What type of text is this?

This is a classic narrative poem. It tells the story of a dashing highwayman who is in love with Bess, the landlord's daughter. She also has another admirer, Tim the ostler, who overhears a conversation between Bess and the highwayman in which the highwayman tells her he is going to go 'after a prize' of gold. He promises to return for her sometime the following day. Tim tips off King George's men, who come to the inn, tie up and gag Bess and lie in wait for the highwayman. Julie actually read this poem in two parts with a Year 5 class and stopped at this point to encourage a discussion about possible endings to the 'story'. It is very tense and dramatic and the children could not wait to find out what actually happened. One girl said 'Well, I'm going to look on the Internet tonight to find out what happens!' It appeals to girls and boys – the boys see a hero in the highwayman and the girls immediately latch onto the tragedy of the love story. Anyway, to cut a long narrative poem short, Bess dies to save the highwayman and then he is killed by King George's men!

The rhythm of a poem is very important. If we look at the first verse (the other verses follow the same pattern):

> The wind was a torrent of darkness among the gusty trees,
> The moon was a ghostly galleon tossed upon cloudy seas,
> The road was a ribbon of moonlight over the purple moor,
> And the highwayman came riding –
>   Riding – riding –
> The highwayman came riding up to the old inn-door.

The verse is split into two distinct parts: the first three lines and the second three lines. The first three lines have a regular rhythm of 15 syllables per line. If you maintain this rhythm when reading the verse, emphasis is automatically placed on the word *riding* with a slightly extended pause where the dash appears. This simulates the rhythm of a horse galloping along. Children can visualise this image of a galloping horse when they read it.

The final three lines of each verse either emphasise the main points or take you on to the next point in the story, for example:

> He loved the landlord's daughter
>   The landlord's red-lipped daughter;
>   Dumb as a dog he listened, and he heard the robber say –

Characters are developed by description, action and dialogue as in a story. Ask the children to describe the highwayman in their own words, to compare the characters of the highwayman and the ostler, and to consider the relationship between Bess and the highwayman.

Sentences and words

Each line in the poem begins with a capital letter. This is typical of traditional poetry. A range of punctuation is used: commas, semicolons, exclamation marks and dashes. Ask the children to consider their effect in the way that the poem is read. There is dialogue in the poem as the highwayman talks to Bess, the layout of which is different to dialogue in a story

– each line begins with a capital letter. Also, the format of the final three lines in the verse is different from the rest. Discuss these differences.

The poem is descriptive and there are many examples of figurative language. The use of metaphor in the first verse to describe the wind, moon and road creates an impression of unpredictable stormy seas by using phrases linked to water, e.g. 'a torrent of darkness' and 'a ghostly galleon tossed upon cloudy seas'. The vocabulary in the poem can be difficult as it is old-fashioned, for example 'ostler', 'breeches', 'harry' and 'brand'. Encourage the children to build up a glossary by trying to define a meaning using contextual and syntactical clues and then checking those meanings using a dictionary.

Activities

The following activities would support the learning objectives for Year 5 Term 2:

- Exploring narrative – through text marking. Ask the children to highlight the key points in the plot, the characters and the setting (use three different-coloured pens). The children can then rewrite the poem as a story.
- Character descriptions – ask the children to describe and compare the highwayman and ostler in their own words. Encourage them to refer to the text to support their opinion.
- Wanted poster – discuss the character of the highwayman, his appearance, what he may have done in the past and what he is about to do. Why would King George's men want to capture him? What information would you include on a wanted poster? The children can then go on to make their own posters for a display.
- Playscripts – work with a group of children to turn a retelling of the poem as a story into a play. This could then be performed.
- Role play – allocate a character from the poem to each of the children in your group. They can then question each other about their actions and feelings in role. For example, Bess could ask Tim the ostler 'Why did you tell King George's men?' Your role would be to act as a facilitator and encourage relevant questions. Why not take on a character yourself?

Non-fiction

In Chapter 3, we pointed out the large range of non-fiction texts that children have to become familiar with at Key Stage 2. Reading non-fiction texts can present children with a number of problems in that they may have to:

● Adopt the special reading techniques of skimming and scanning to locate information. These skills are also useful for finding information on the Internet (see Chapter 7).

● Access the part of the text they need by using an index.

● Be able to decipher technical vocabulary and jargon.

● Contend with more formal language.

● Consider the credibility of both the source and content of the information.

When you are tackling non-fiction in the classroom, a large proportion of your time will be spent working with children to help them to overcome these difficulties.

Skimming and scanning

How many times have you heard a teacher say 'I told you not to copy from the book'? On one occasion, a teacher said this to a Year 4 boy during a history lesson. The teacher was exasperated and the boy was totally confused. When the teacher asked him why he had copied the boy replied 'Because I didn't know what else to do. How do you write about the children being evacuated without copying?' Hopefully this situation is not as common as it once was because the problems the little boy faced can be overcome by teaching the skills of:

● formulating questions;

● skimming and scanning;

● note-making.

The children can then apply these specific skills to reading for information to support other National Curriculum subjects.

What is skimming?

The idea of skimming is to locate a very general area. So, if you were reading a book about the body to find out about how the eye worked, you would skim down the index page until you reached the E entries.

What is scanning?

Scanning is more thorough than skimming. Once you have located the E's by skimming you would then scan more slowly to find the specific word 'eye'.

Activities to help children acquire these skills

- Spot the 's' – give the children a paragraph of a non-fiction text such as a report and ask them to count up the number of times the letter 's' (or a letter of your choice) appears on the page. This could become a timed activity as the children get more proficient.
- Finding answers – pose the children a specific question, for example: When did Henry VIII come to the throne? The children can then scan a relevant page of text for the answer. Point out the key words in the question such as 'when' (the children will then know to look for the date).

Note-making

If children are taught how to note down the key points of information from a text they can then use this information to write their own sentences using their own connectives etc. but in the relevant text structure, for example an explanation for 'How an aeroplane flies'. Children should be encouraged to make notes from Year 3 Term 2 when they have to 'identify key words, phrases or sentences in reading'. This should continue throughout Key Stage 2.

Activities to assist note-making skills:

- You can do this by creating a simple scenario, for example a friend writing to another friend to say what time he will pick him up for football training. Write a simple letter but include lots of irrelevant information:

Dear Sam,
I bet you are really excited about football training on <u>Friday</u>, I know I am! We will pick you up from <u>your house at 6pm</u>. My mum will probably be driving but it might be my dad. You will need your <u>kit, goal-keeping gloves</u>, <u>a bottle of water and a waterproof coat</u>.
See you then.
Tom

Discuss the purpose of such a note, i.e. to give time and place of pick-up and what the child will need to take. Ask the children to underline the words that are most important. It should look something like the one above. The children can then rewrite it as a note.

- Older children can do a similar activity with a selected non-fiction text, assuming they are using a prepared sheet and not the book itself! If they do use a book text they can list a series of bullet points.

- Making graphic representations of notes can help children to remember facts, chronological order etc. Work with the children to produce flow charts for example. Julie recently encouraged a reluctant reader to draw around his hand and note five pieces of information about 'sharks' (one in each finger!). He enjoyed this activity as it restricted what he had to do and so he felt less overwhelmed.

For further information on note-making see work by Bobby Neate (2001) (see 'Further reading' at the end of this chapter).

Technical vocabulary and jargon

Learn about the Body Steve Parker

What type of text is this?

This book is described as a project book. It contains information which is presented as:

- reports;
- explanations (describing how specific body parts work);

- procedures (instructions for activities such as 'Making a Breath Machine').

The reports on each subject area, for example 'Bones and Joints', are simple and the illustrations are colourful, including drawings and a microscopic view of the inside of a bone. They help the reader to make sense of the text. A number of the diagrams are labelled or have a small amount of specific information written next to them under a bold subheading, for example:

Types of joints
The elbow and knee are hinge joints

Sentences and words – 'Bones and Joints'

Typical of a report, the text is written in the present tense in order to tell the reader how something is. A number of the sentences have the same beginning: 'A bone...' or 'Bones...' This constantly reminds the reader what the section is about. The diagram labelling provides examples of shortened phrases, e.g. 'Bone in finger' instead of 'a bone in the finger'. The vocabulary is technical, e.g. *collagen, cartilage* and *phosphates*.

Activities

These activities will support the National Literacy Strategy non-fiction objectives from Year 3 to Year 6:

- Finding answers – as previously suggested, ask the children to find the answers to five specific questions relating to the report, e.g. how many bones are there in the skeleton? Ask them how they found the answers. If the answers were not in the main body of the report how did they know which part of the page to look at?
- Gathering information – use one of the methods suggested earlier in the chapter to make notes on 'Bones and Joints'. Encourage the children to think about key words and phrases only.
- Writing reports – work with the children to structure their notes and write their own report.

- Using an index – give the children a collection of topics featured in the index. Ask them to use the index to locate the appropriate page number.

- Diagram labelling – work with the children to draw a skeleton and label the main features using the correct vocabulary and clear lines.

- Improper instructions – one of the projects may be used to examine instructions. To read instructions, the children need to be clear that putting them in the correct order is vital. Reproduce a set of instructions in the wrong order or omit a step. Ask the children to follow the instructions and then establish where they went wrong. Work with the children to rewrite the correct instructions.

Summary

In this chapter we have discussed:

- How reading is different at Key Stage 2.
- The different teaching approaches and resources.
- Specific examples of a range of texts at text, sentence and word level and a range of ideas for activities in the classroom.

Further reading

Carter, D. (1998) *Teaching Poetry in the Primary School.* London: David Fulton Publishers.

Gamble, N. and Yates, S. (2002) *Exploring Children's Literature: Teaching the Language and Reading of Fiction.* London: Paul Chapman Publishing.

Morpurgo, Michael (1987) *Conker.* London: Heinemann.

Neate, B. (2001) 'Notemaking techniques for young children', in J. Evans (ed.) *The Writing Classroom.* London: David Fulton Publishers (esp. 116–26).

Parker, Steve (1999) *The Body.* London: Dorling Kindersley.

Reid, D. and Bentley, D. (eds) (1996) *Reading On! Developing Reading at Key Stage 2.* Leamington Spa: Scholastic.

Chapter 7

Reading non-book and electronic texts

The term 'non-book' covers a multitude of publications (often referred to as media texts) from comics and newspapers to promotional and advertising leaflets. Electronic texts are those that can be transmitted through an electronic medium such as a computer or mobile phone, and therefore cover websites, CD-ROMs and text messages etc.

In this chapter we will examine the features of non-book narrative and information texts by considering the features of each text type and the skills and knowledge that adults and children need to make sense of them. The text types covered will include:

● comic strips;
● promotional leaflets;
● Internet/websites.

The approach to reading these text types can be applied to other 'media' and book texts. For example:

● comic strips and graphic books;
● promotional leaflets and advertisements;
● Internet websites and CD-ROMs, newspapers and magazines.

If you are working with children at Key Stage 2 you will be using this full range of text types. This chapter will offer ideas for reading-based activities that you may use with the children.

The relevance of media texts

From an early age, children are aware of the visual impact of signs, symbols and logos. This was evident in Julie's son (now aged 10), who at the age of 2^1/$_2$ would shout 'Ah, someone cares!' each time they drove past a Boots lorry on the motorway. What he was shouting was, of course, the Boots' TV advertising slogan at the time, thus suggesting his ability to both recognise and link a logo with a product despite a lack of understanding of meaning.

There is no doubt that our world is one of visual stimulus and developing communications and technologies. Children need to be made aware of how to handle texts that belong to this new age and understand how language is being adapted to different situations – after all 'what was basic literacy two decades ago is not compatible with current needs' (Craggs 1992: 3). Making sense of so-called non-literary texts requires enhanced reading skills as the reader must learn a set of codes or conventions, and in many cases must deconstruct the text (i.e. take it apart and consider *why* the author created it in a particular way) to interpret a correct meaning. Therefore, it is important for us, as adults, to be aware of changing language conventions.

Comics

Comics are probably the most familiar non-electronic media text type available to children. Our memories are of piles of comics being placed on the desk by the teacher during wet playtime. This act was representative of the attitude towards comics in that they were, and still are to a certain extent, seen as a bit of fun – not a proper read with any educational value. The fact is, however, that they are very cleverly put together and follow their own generic structure and format. It is necessary to know how to read a comic in order to fully understand its content. This knowledge can then be applied to the increasingly popular genre of children's books: the graphic book.

The structure of a comic strip

A comic strip is split into boxes or 'frames'. Within each frame the story is developed in three ways:

● *Graphics* – the drawings are visually descriptive showing actions etc. They are crucial in providing information about characters and setting as written words are limited.

● *Speech and thought bubbles* – the story is told mainly through dialogue in the form of speech/thought bubbles. There is a range of bubble types to indicate whispering (a whisper bubble is like a speech bubble but with a dotted line), shouting, thinking etc.

● *Story narration and time-lapse boxes* – the frame is often split to show a small box at the top which either outlines the story, provides a link or details a setting.

Therefore, the ability to enjoy a comic strip is dependent primarily upon the reader being able to read and interpret a series of signs and symbols.

Comic strip language

Generally there is a tendency towards a more colloquial informal language, mainly due to the fact that the largest proportion of the written language is in the form of dialogue. The titles of each story or strip can be likened to a newspaper article in that they often involve puns, alliteration or rhyme. By studying a specific comic strip in more detail, it is possible to identify the features of structure and style. In the more traditional comics the language is often dated.

The Beano (No 3216, March 6th 2004)

This is a classic comic generally considered to be aimed, primarily, at boys. The main characters are children who tend to be anarchic, showing little respect for adults or authority. At text level it is important to discuss actions, attitudes and behaviours mainly because a typical comic strip will challenge our own cultural and moral values by condoning what the government would deem to be antisocial behaviours!

Dennis the Menace and Minnie the Minx are probably two of the most well-known comic characters and both feature in this publication.

Minnie the Minx feature (from the above issue)

The title

The definition of the word 'minx' is: 'a pert, sly, or playful girl' (*The Oxford Compact English Dictionary* 1996). This immediately conjures up an image of her character and combined with the use of both alliteration (the repeated 'm' sound at the beginning of each noun) and assonance (the repeated short vowel sound 'i'), does indeed make it memorable!

The plot and characters

In brief, Minnie is taken to Crumbly Castle, the alliterative 'crumbly' suggesting its state of repair. The first frame makes it clear that she does not want to be there. The plot is developed by Minnie stealing sausages from an out-of-place burger bar and dropping a cannon ball on the foot of a museum official, in keeping with character expectations. However, the final frames show Minnie being caught and humiliated in the stocks, her anger at which is made clear through facial expression and dialogue as she refers to those taking part in her punishment as 'dirty rotters'.

As with any narrative text, actions and dialogue are key to building up character descriptions. Comics have the added advantage of a picture description. Minnie can be seen wearing a striped jumper, similar to that of her fellow *Beano* star, Dennis the Menace. This is an example of graphic intertextuality – the readers' expectations of both characters will be the same.

In this feature, the yellow time-lapse box at the top of selected frames contains a single connective, e.g. 'then', 'shortly' and 'next', to add cohesion to the text by ordering it chronologically.

Word choices and sentence structure

Words are chosen carefully for maximum impact, and because the emphasis is on dialogue, the written syntax is the same as that of spontaneous speech. In the first frame, the more formal dialogue of Minnie's father, who says, 'Going around this old castle will be jolly interesting, Minnie', is contrasted sharply with Minnie's more colloquial response. 'Hmph! Borin' ol' place is deserted.' The final letters of 'boring' and 'old' are replaced with apostrophes. The author has chosen to miss the final sounds from words to suggest that a young person is speaking and in this case the method works! The reader is immediately aware that these words are spoken by a younger person without having to look at the supporting graphics for confirmation. The adult characters all tend to speak in complete sentences with a more formal tone.

Despite this clear difference in the adult and child language within the text, in general the language is very dated. Examples are 'dirty rotters' and the use of the word 'hooter' to represent a nose. Interestingly, this use of dated language does not appear to affect children's enjoyment of the comic. In fact, Julie's son found it very amusing to refer to everyone's nose as their 'hooter' for weeks after reading this strip!

The text also contains a number of invented words such as 'squoylch' which could be derived from 'squash' and 'squelch' and so is immediately identifiable. Others need to be read in conjunction with the graphics to give a more clear meaning, for example 'GNNOINK!' The capitalisation and punctuation show that it is a shouted exclamation but seeing the picture of the character having his nose squashed immediately causes the reader to focus on the 'oink' part of the word which has connotations with pigs and snouts! Children will have lots of fun making up their own nonsense words.

Sounds also play a huge part in this comic strip. From the noises characters are making to the noise made by instruments from the torture chamber and sausages 'sizzling'. This, like most of the words used in the feature to suggest noise, is an example of onomatopoeia, but it is also a particularly interesting example of *suggested* alliteration 'sausages sizzling on a sword', created through graphics as the only written word is 'sizzle'.

Graphics

Using the above illustration as an example, we can see a wide range of graphic devices being used in both the pictures and typeset. There is a standard speech bubble to identify dialogue but the most interesting features are the three different ways noise is represented

- jagged lines;
- bold type;
- bubble type and capitalisation.

In each case, the text is followed by an exclamation mark which suggests a display of emotion in each case – 'oy' suggests anger, 'zoom' determination and 'sizzle' is for humorous effect. The word 'zoom' also suggests movement, apparent by its increasing size from left to right.

The knowledge and understanding of visual literacy needed to read and appreciate *The Beano* can be applied to all comic features including graphic books; some websites have also adopted this style.

Activities

You may find these activities useful. They would lend themselves well as support for the learning objectives for Year 4 Term 2:

- Story sequencing – encourage the children to read the pictures without any bubbles or link words. Discuss with the children how they decided on the order and what clues they looked for.

- Now you're talking (1) – give the children a couple of frames with empty bubbles. Encourage the children to study the pictures and decide what the character might be saying. They can then write the dialogue in the bubbles. This is a great introduction to work on punctuating dialogue.

- Now you're talking (2) – the children can compare their own work in the above activity with the words in the actual comic strip. Encourage the children to think about whether or not they have a similar storyline to the original? Why are they the same/different?

- Comic comparisons – compare the content and style of *The Beano* with a girl's comic such as *Girl Talk*. Look at layout, use of colour, font, graphics, stories and features. This activity appeals to both girls and boys and usually results in a heated debate about which is best!

Tourist information promotional leaflets

Promotional leaflets provide a most colourful and accessible route into persuasive writing. Tourist attraction leaflets are readily available and offer opportunities to compare layout and language. All such leaflets can be broken down into three main parts, all serving a particular purpose: cover, centre and back page. The cover is designed to attract the attention of the target audience and persuade them to pick up the leaflet – an eye-catching picture and persuasive text work together to achieve this. The centre of the leaflet will give some information about the place itself, often in the form of a labelled map, bullet points or headings. The back of the leaflet will contain essential information, for example opening times, cost, facilities, location etc.

The Blue Planet Aquarium (www.blueplanetaquarium.com)

What type of text is this?

This is a persuasive text promoting the Blue Planet Aquarium, a large indoor attraction in the North West of England. It is set out in typical leaflet fashion, as previously described, but there are some noticeable omissions which will be considered later.

The leaflet itself is of a standard length and width with three folds and a tear-off strip. Size is important for tourist information leaflets as they are generally distributed to hotels etc. where they are displayed in a wire 'pouch' so they have to fit! The cover has an eye-catching picture of a very happy-looking family surrounded by sea creatures, the most impressive of which is a huge shark. The picture provides a lot of information by suggesting that:

● The target audience is a family (they stand out because of the use of colour for their clothes in what is otherwise a mainly blue and yellow colour scheme).

● The exhibits are very impressive and out of the ordinary.

Both the picture and the written words play on the fear aspect, suggesting that visitors will come close to danger, the real danger being sharks (the picture shows a shark fin brushing over the top of Mum's head). She is still smiling though, suggesting that the danger will be encountered in a safe environment! The theme of 'fear' runs throughout and the leaflet unfolds to present the potential visitor with the ultimate challenge: 'Get closer if you dare!'

The centre of the leaflet presents the hard sell aspect: it wants to encourage both new and return visitors. The first piece of information presented to the reader, as the leaflet is unfolded, is aimed at the return visitor. It concerns a new exhibit, the otters, and is gentle and cute in sharp contrast to the rest of the text – thus suggesting a new experience. The otters are in fact presented as 'delightful creatures' whereas everything else is rather scary!

In its effort to persuade you to visit, the leaflet has a number of interesting features:

- The experience will not only be entertaining but educational due to the staff's professional expertise. '**Marine biologists** will tell you about the amazing fish' and '**divers** hand-feed the sharks'.
- The map on the back of the leaflet shows the Blue Planet Aquarium and the major motorway and trunk roads only, which end in an arrow-head pointing in the direction of a major city or region, e.g. Preston, Leeds, Birmingham, North Wales etc. This suggests to the reader that it is easily accessible to the Midlands as well as the North West, therefore distance is no barrier!

What is not included is the cost of admission for a single visit. It does provide the cost of annual passes which range from £19.30 for a child to £85.00 for a two adult/two children family pass. This information is provided in a tear-off strip for easy reference and with a box to complete for further information. This approach is, in its own way, persuasive and suggests:

- There must be lots to see as visitors must buy these annual passes.
- It is expensive and so must be good!
- The cost of a single day pass will not be as much and so will seem cheap by comparison!

Throughout the text, information is presented under very bold headings. The use of photographs not only makes it visually stimulating but reinforces the information provided about the target audience and overall experience. In fact, at the top of the leaflet are the words '*THE ULTIMATE UNDERWATER ADVENTURE!*' This is written in capital letters in a blue/lilac colour within a yellow halo effect, almost suggesting visitors will have an enlightening experience.

Sentences

There are numerous examples of verbs in their imperative (command) form, e.g. '*Make sure* you don't miss a thing!' and '*See* huge sharks from one of the world's longest underwater viewing tunnels.' This particular sentence offers the opportunity to examine superlative adjectives such as 'longest'. Other examples in the text include 'largest' ('Our new otter enclosure is one of the largest in the UK') and 'biggest' ('We've got the biggest in the UK').

There are examples of persuasive phrases such as 'not to be missed' and sentences like 'It's a great day out, whatever the weather' and 'It's an experience you'll never forget.' The text also poses a number of questions such as 'What does it feel like to stroke a dogfish?' The only way to find out of course is to do it! Therefore, the purpose of the questions is to entice the reader into visiting the aquarium to find the answers.

The tone of the text is informal, addressing each reader in turn (after all, such a leaflet is made for sharing and passing around the prospective visiting party). It addresses the reader as 'you' and the informal tone leads to a number of examples of elision. For example, 'you will' is shortened to 'you'll' and 'do not' to 'don't'. This demonstrates the use of an apostrophe to mark a contraction which is expected in informal writing and speech.

Word choice

The top of the front cover shows an example of alliteration, 'The *ultimate underwater* adventure' and, as with a newspaper headline, it grabs attention. The word 'ultimate' is incredibly persuasive, suggesting that it should not be missed. Other examples of persuasive vocabulary in the leaflet are 'spellbound', 'awesome' and 'brilliant'. The exhibits are described using interesting adjectives. Frogs appear with *vivid* colours and there are *graceful* rays and *fearsome* sharks. It is interesting to think about why the author has used the apparently contradictory vocabulary 'pretty deadly' to describe the frogs. Pretty, as in attractive and pretty, as in quite. Both definitions would fit the context. Ask the children what they think the author intended.

Activities

The following activities are useful as they support the National Literacy Strategy learning objectives for Year 4 Term 3 through to Year 6 Term 1:

- Persuasive phrases – the children read a selection of tourist information leaflets and identify the persuasive words and phrases (these can be cut out and mounted to make a display). Encourage the children to discuss the reasoning behind their selections in order to assess their understanding of the task. You can feed your findings back to the teacher.

- Target audience – ask the children to examine a range of leaflet front covers. They can then complete a comparison table in which they write the name of the attraction, a brief description of the cover, possible target audience and reasons for this. Julie carried out this activity with a Year 5 class who compared the bold Blue Planet Aquarium leaflet with that of Ness Botanical Gardens which had a pastel impressionist-style illustration of wild flowers. They agreed that the aquarium was for families with young children and the gardens were definitely an attraction for 'old people', because the picture was like a 'birthday card that you give to your Gran!'

- Creating a promotional leaflet – you can work with younger children to recreate a leaflet they are familiar with. Alternatively, the children can make a leaflet for an attraction of their choice. This is also a good way of recording a school trip – Julie's Year 5 class produced a leaflet to record their 'Victorian Christmas' afternoon at a National Trust property.

The Internet

Most of us use the Internet regularly and have come to understand its importance for finding information. However, reading web pages can sometimes be confusing and this can create problems for children who have to learn to select and discard information. You can help them with the process by being aware both of the problems they will encounter and the differences between web and conventional book texts.

The BBC TV website

The address

This is popular not only with schools because of its educational value but also with adults and children in the home. It is important to consider the syntax or grammar of the address itself and how punctuation terminology has evolved through usage. This does, however, present you with a great opportunity to encourage children to think about and discuss punctuation.

www.bbc.co.uk

Users of the Internet know that 'www' is an acronym for World Wide Web which is followed by a full stop, referred to as a 'dot'. The dot is not recognised as a full stop in this situation and is an example of the evolution of punctuation. The 'forward slash' is another example of this as inexperienced web users will often refer to it in a more traditional way as an oblique.

www.bbc.co.uk/cbbc

The letters in the BBC's web address are written in lower case, despite the fact that capital letters are usually seen at the beginning of each word. This is typical of all web addresses: letters (including the first letters of proper nouns) are generally written in lower case. It is important to point this out to the children.

The homepage

The majority of websites will have a homepage which works in a similar way to the contents page and introduction of a non-fiction reference book. It will provide information about the site (introduction) and links to other parts of the site (contents). The main differences between a website and a conventional text are:

- layout;
- inclusion of advertising material;
- moving and static graphics.

The BBC's homepage (March 2004)

Web pages tend to be very busy with lots going on and the BBC's homepage is no exception! Learning to **navigate** a website and **discard** irrelevant information in order to find a relevant page is a crucial part of the reading process that a child will not generally encounter with a more conventional print text. It is in this area that you will have to provide most support.

Layout

This is a rather confusing page as it defies the convention of reading left to right! Instead it is set out in columns, rather like a newspaper. Information is ordered in such a way that the user is drawn to the right-hand side of the page as this offers the only real structure in the form of a 'directory'.

- **Directory** – this is in two parts: (1) the alphabet presented in capital letters, e.g. click on 'A' for information about *The Archers* and (2) an index of subjects presented in bold type and ordered alphabetically to allow the user to select a specific subject area, e.g. History.

- **Search facility** – this is located at the top, left-hand side of the page. Most homepages will have this facility allowing the user to type in a keyword and search the site's index. The user can then discard the other information on the page. This facility can be sited anywhere on the page but is usually found at the top right-hand corner. Note: it is important to encourage children to locate the search facility and use it as it maintains a focus and stops time being wasted. I'm sure, like me, you have spent hours searching websites and been distracted because something looked interesting! Keep this in mind.

- **Advertising** – the advertising is limited to forthcoming TV programmes and BBC products. The main advertisement is in the form of a captivating photographic image with a simple question: 'What does the world think of God?' This is followed by 'Find out tonight on BBC2'.

- **Symbols** – the BBC uses a variety of symbols. There are universally accepted symbols to show weather conditions in London, e.g. a yellow sun on a blue background representing 'sunny' on 26th February 2004, and others that would, without explanation, be known only to users of the products (see below for some examples).

Broadband   **CBBC**   **CBeebies**

This set of symbols and others like them are known as 'icons'. This is an example of how language and word usage evolves (the word 'icon' having been traditionally associated with sacred images not computer symbols). Of course, the excessive use of symbols across all areas of information technology is another example of the importance of understanding visual literacy. The symbols on this homepage are static, i.e. they remain in position.

Word choice and grammar

Like a newspaper, the information is given in a series of headlines, e.g.

N Korea 'makes nuclear offer'

The 'N' is an example of an abbreviation of North and there is correct use of capitalisation for the proper nouns. The sentence does not end with a full stop and this is a feature of any headline. There are inverted commas punctuating the quotation element and this quotation, combined with the fact that it is written in the present tense suggesting breaking news, has the effect of making the reader want to read on and find out more.

Children's BBC (www.bbc.co.uk/cbbc)

The homepage layout for Children's BBC contains less written text and more icons. There is a static contents listing on the right-hand side of the page, i.e. it remains permanently displayed even if the reader scrolls down the page. This is helpful as contents of indexes that do move as you scroll down the page can be problematic because you have to remember what has gone before. There is a moving image at the top of the page: the CBBC logo and a synonymous green 'blob' move across the top of the page. This serves the purpose of both amusing the reader and confirming that the desired page/area has been accessed. However, it is an example of web page material that can otherwise be ignored.

Activities

- Features – work with the children to read a homepage, like the BBC example above, and discuss the similarities between it and conventional books. You could print out a copy of the homepage and the children could highlight familiar features through text marking. Discuss the importance of ignoring moving images and reading for a search box. This keeps the reader focused on the research task.

- Finding facts challenge – the teacher may ask the children to research a specific topic, for example the water cycle. Ask half of your group to find information using conventional books and the other half to use the Internet. The children should note what they did to find the information, e.g. use a contents page etc. Which of your group found the information most quickly? Ask the children to discuss possible reasons for this and to compare approaches.

- True or false – as with any information text the children must learn to establish the credibility of the source. Give the children a selection of websites (choose carefully) for them to review. How would they know if the information was true? Encourage them to look for an author, date of publication and a date when the website was last updated.

Summary

In this chapter we have discussed:

- The relevance of media texts in the primary classroom.
- The features of comic strips.
- Tourist information leaflets and persuasive writing.
- Reading for information using the Internet.
- Suggestions for activities in the classroom.

Further reading

Craggs, C. (1992) *Media Education in the Primary School.* London: Routledge.

Harpley, A. (1990) *Bright Ideas Media Education.* Leamington Spa: Scholastic.

Chapter 8

Assessment and monitoring of reading

Reading is, quite rightly, considered to be at the very heart of the primary curriculum. The reasons for that can be stated quite simply:

- The children's progress in learning to read will have an enormous influence on how they tackle almost everything else in school.

- The government has placed literacy (reading and writing) at the heart of its drive to raise standards in schools.

- Looking further ahead, becoming 'a reader' in the ways we have defined it in this book is a life-enhancing experience in so many ways.

More than for anything else that they do, schools have to account for their success in reading and writing to all their various stakeholders: politicians, the media, LEAs, inspectors, governors, parents and, most importantly, the children themselves. It seems very likely therefore that you will be expected to play a part in ensuring that every child is encouraged to make progress and receives appropriate and adequate support for any problems that arise. This means helping the teacher to monitor and assess on a regular, perhaps even a daily basis. You're more likely to be directly involved in these formative and diagnostic assessments than in the summative assessments that take place at the end of a key stage.

What is being tested?

We hope that we have convinced you in this book that reading is a complex, multifaceted activity. It follows from this that it must be quite a detailed task to find out if a child is making good progress. One of the perennial problems in schools is the tug between wanting quick tests which are easy to administer and the need for detailed data which really define what the child can do and where s/he needs to go next. This data can be time-consuming for a teacher to collect so having a teaching assistant to help will be invaluable.

Let us remind you of some of the facets of reading which have been discussed in these pages:

- Accuracy in decoding written symbols.
- Fluency.
- Speed.
- Choosing an appropriate reading strategy for the situation the reader is in.
- Responding appropriately to what has been read. This might involve, among other things:
  - evidence of deepening and widening personal experience
  - taking on board new ideas
  - modifying existing ideas
- Developing a taste for new authors and new types of text.

It's a tall order for any one reading test to provide information on all these fronts. Something you need to watch out for is the labelling of children as 'poor readers' – or even as 'good readers' – when the evidence for this labelling is very partial, perhaps the result of one reading test taken on one day. There is a danger of these test results becoming self-fulfilling prophecies.

Broadly speaking, you will find reading tests of two kinds administered in schools: word recognition and comprehension.

Comprehension tests

We have already discussed the weaknesses of some (though by no means all) comprehension tests (see p. 49). Another difficulty is that these tests can be culturally biased. For example, some of the tests take the form of sentence completion activities, where a child chooses a word to complete a sentence from five alternatives. What is required to score highly is actually a wide vocabulary and good general knowledge. Here is an example:

> The bare trees made a lacy pattern against the (summer, empty, wide, blue, wintry) sky.

Not only must this reference to an English winter ('wintry' is the right answer) mean very little to a child recently arrived from Pakistan, but a case could be made out for any of the words fitting into the gap. On one occasion a child chose 'blue'. Does this make him a 'poor reader'?

Word recognition tests

To do well in a word recognition test, such as the Schonell Reading Test, a child must read a series of words out loud. If a word gets a little difficult, the child is asked to sound it out. If s/he can't say what a word is, they go on to the next one. After a fairly straightforward beginning:

tree   little   milk   egg

if the child is good enough at decoding, s/he eventually comes to:

metamorphosis   somnambulist   bibliography   idiosyncrasy

It is not necessary to understand these words or to be able to spell them; merely to be able to say them aloud correctly with the emphasis in the right place.

It is sometimes the case that if a child's results from a word recognition test are compared with those from a comprehension test completed at or around the same time, the results are significantly different. This is because quite different aspects of reading are being tested.

We are well aware that this is only a brief reference to a very complex subject. We are also aware that you are unlikely to be in a position to be able to influence the types of test that may be used in your school. Our aim in mentioning these aspects of testing is first to urge you, when you hear of a child being labelled in respect of his/her reading, to try to find out (tactfully) what the evidence for the judgement is based on. More importantly still, we want to convince you of the vital role that you can play in providing the class teacher with your own evidence of daily achievements, however small, to supplement the more formally gathered evidence.

Miscue analysis

This type of test takes into account the mistakes, or miscues, a child makes when reading a passage aloud. This is done by annotating the words the child misreads with a symbol to denote how the word was misread. Pauses, word omissions and insertions are also taken into account. The symbols used may vary but this example is taken from Wray and Sullivan (1996: 17).

//	pausing
<u>means</u>	underline – sounding out phonetically
~~and~~	crossing out – omission
on /	addition or insertion
make ~~milk~~	substitution
C	self-correction

If you carry out a test like this you may use an overlay on your copy of the passage to mark the results. The miscues will then be analysed by the teacher who will look for patterns that will enable her to establish the child's approach to reading. It is also a good idea to discuss the story with the child and ask for a retelling of events in order to help you to feed back information about the child's understanding of the book. An example of miscue analysis used in schools is the English Key Stage 1 SAT and the Key Stage 2 English Task for those children expected to reach Level 2/3 at the end of Year 6. It is a good diagnostic test but it is time-consuming as appropriate texts have to be carefully chosen in addition to actually administering the test.

Informal observations

It should be possible over a period of time to gather some useful evidence simply by watching the children at work. The teacher might have asked you to focus on a particular child or you could set aside a regular period of time, say 15 minutes a day, to do this kind of observation around the class as a whole. It's just as important to observe the good readers as the strugglers – they need to be moved on too. Furthermore, their behaviour can often give you a lot of useful information about children and their reading. Here are some pointers to look out for:

- *The number of times a child chooses to read (as distinct from being required to).* We talked in Chapter 1 about confident readers knowing 'what reading is good for'. Depending, of course, on the ages of the children you are working with, you might notice them going back to a story the teacher has read or doing some reading connected with a topic that has come up in class, a hobby or just something that has caught their eye etc.

- *Children exhibiting a range of reading behaviours.* We have referred throughout the book to reading being a range of different behaviours from skimming and scanning, searching for some specific information using indexes and so on, to the slow savouring of a poem or perhaps enjoying saying it – or shouting it – for the fun of the sounds the words make. Check whether, once they've been introduced to them, the children use this range of behaviours.

- *Children who are struggling.* Signs to look out for include the child who never chooses to read, the child who is continually gazing around or wanting to change to a different book, or who is flipping across a lot of material on screen or distracting others who are trying to access something. Even during shared reading sessions, such children may find it hard to contribute or even to maintain concentration. Group reading sessions too should show up a range of problems. It might be that the vocabulary is too difficult or the syntactic structure of the text is causing a problem. The child may be overusing phonic strategies, forgetting or not able to use context and syntactic cues. Obviously these observations should be passed on to the teacher as a matter of urgency so that some more diagnostic work can be done.

- *Children reading too slowly – or too quickly.* This takes us back to the need to employ a range of reading strategies. Children need to know what speed is appropriate for the specific reading task. In today's world, it is something of a curse to be a slow and plodding reader, however dedicated. There's just too much to read. Some children 'sub-vocalise' – if you watch carefully you will see them silently mouthing the words. This too takes much too long. On the other hand, some children rush through every text at the speed of light, completely missing some of those subtler inferences and levels of meaning that we have talked about.

Talking to children

Throughout this book we have made the assumption that part of your role will be to share books with individuals and groups. These conversations can also be used to make informal assessments.

- As the children read, you will have an ideal opportunity to notice the range of cues they employ when they are in difficulties. (It's hard to know what is going on when they are reading fluently!)

- You will be in a good position to explore the quality of their response to what has been read. Some children don't want to make a response at all – they just want to get on to the next page! This may be justified if the text is very exciting, but you should be suspicious if it happens all the time.

- You may be able to talk to the children about the influence their reading is having on their writing, or in drama or a spoken language activity. No assessment can be done in isolation from everything else that is happening – especially all the other language activities.

- There may be a reason why a child appears to do little reading in class and you could probe this further. Do they prefer to read in another language? Do they read more at home because it's quieter and they have somewhere to curl up comfortably? Do they read elsewhere because of a hobby or interest that can't be followed up via the school's resources? Maybe the school could support some of these other reading interests – perhaps by organising reading groups in other languages.

Always make sure that you give the children plenty of feedback and encouragement. Really listen carefully to what they are telling you and, of course, think carefully about what you observe. It may be that some of the barriers to some children's enthusiasm can be overcome: by providing a wider range of reading material, for example, or somewhere comfortable to sit and read. If you seem to be hearing that reading is a 'girlie' activity then it might be possible to arrange for some male visitors to read with the children and talk about their own reading interests.

Self-assessment

Finding out how children see themselves as readers can be an invaluable aid to progression and motivation. You can do this by asking questions such as:

● What do you think makes a good reader?

● What are your strengths as a reader?

● Do you think of yourself as a good reader?

● How could you make yourself an even better reader?

● Which are your favourite authors and why?

● What do you do if you don't understand a word?

● What problems do you think people might have when they are learning to read?

● Which of these problems do you have most trouble with?

● Why do you think it is important to be able to read?

You may record oral responses to the questions or you may help children to complete a questionnaire. This activity was carried out recently in a Year 5/6 class and the results provided an interesting insight into the children's attitudes and approaches to reading. One girl felt that reading with 'ecxpreshion' was what made a good reader and that this was a problem for her because she didn't always understand what she read. She did, however, enjoy reading and Jacqueline Wilson was her favourite author. Interestingly, all of the poorer readers were most concerned with this idea of expression and reading aloud. They were all keen to 'sound right' and appear competent. As a result of this self-assessment, the teacher can now work on focused comprehension activities with this group of children with less emphasis on decoding words.

▧ Records

What kinds of notes do you make, how and for whom? The last point is the easiest.

For whom?

Mostly, your notes will be for the class teacher's use but you may be asked to share something with another teacher or a parent. Obviously it goes without saying that no assessment information should be discussed outside the school walls.

You may find that regular informal chats can feed into the teacher's record-keeping. On the other hand, it may not always be easy to get together in which case written notes may be helpful.

What should you write down?

Tick boxes or shading are quick but they don't give enough information – comments in your own words are much more informative. You don't, however, have to reinvent the wheel. You will find that the school, perhaps following LEA guidelines, has worked out the levels children are expected to achieve at each stage and these will help to inform what you write. You may be fed up with hearing us say it, but just to remind you again – because a child is seven doesn't mean s/he can do everything in the National Curriculum for Key Stage 1. However, provided that you treat them as a rough guide, published lists of what's expected at each stage of a child's development as a reader can be useful:

● Beginning at three years old, the earliest assessment involves parents too, of course. The first set of observations is carried out no later than seven weeks from a child's entry into nursery. At the end of the nursery year, they are passed on to the Reception class. They then inform the statutory baseline assessment completed within the first seven weeks of the

Reception class. Eventually the records go to the Year 1 teacher for information.

● From Year 1 onwards, you will have the National Curriculum attainment targets to guide you and again, you are likely to find more detailed LEA or school statements of attainment. Currently, National Assessment Tests (often referred to as SATs) are still being held in England and you may find it useful to read through some of the marking guidelines from past years to give you some idea of what's expected at each level.

● It's just as important to note what a child does well as it is to record what they have difficulty with. As you become more confident, try to make your notes as precise as you possibly can, highlighting a child's enterprise, for example, in working out the meaning of a tricky line. 'James read well today' or 'Samantha struggled with this' are not really going to help very much. James wonders just what it was that pleased you and Samantha needs some specific help with vowel digraphs.

Summary

In this chapter we have discussed:

● The aspects of reading we want to test.
● Types of test that teaching assistants might be involved in (semi-formal)
● Informal gathering of evidence.
● Keeping records of reading achievement.

Further reading

Bentley, D., Gray, D. and Chamberlain, R. (1999) *The Really Practical Guide to Primary English.* London: Nelson Thornes.

Mallet, M. (2002) *The Primary English Encyclopaedia: The Heart of the Curriculum.* London: David Fulton Publishers.

Wray, D. and Sullivan, M. (1996) *Literacy Assessment: Key Stage 2.* Leamington Spa: Scholastic.

Wray, D., Medwell, J. and Sullivan, M. (1996) *Literacy Assessment: Key Stage 1*. Leamington Spa: Scholastic.

Index